SECOND-HAND SUCCESS

HOW TO TURN DISCARDS INTO DOLLARS

JORDAN L COOPER

Loompanics Unlimited
Port Townsend, Washington

This book is sold for information purposes only. Neither the author nor the publisher will be held accountable for the use or misuse of the information contained in this book.

Published by:
Loompanics Unlimited
P.O. Box 1197
Port Townsend, WA 98368
Loompanics Unlimited is a division of Loompanics Enterprises, Inc.

ISBN 1-55950-122-7
Library of Congress Catalog Card Number 94-79873

Contents

To Peggy and Frank Funk

The world's greatest neighbors,
on the Verde or anywhere else,
and two of God's special people.

INTRODUCTION

Each year, Americans throw away millions, perhaps even billions, of dollars. Unlike the government, which deliberately throws away billions each year, the average American does it inadvertently.

Our annual output of garbage would bury 26,000 football fields 10 feet deep. Californians alone produce enough garbage to bury the entire city of San Francisco knee-deep in waste. Of the 70 billion aluminum cans included in this volume, about 60 percent find their way into recycling bins. While some people merely pitch their cans into containers clearly marked for that purpose, others save them to sell at recycling centers. These range from winos looking for drinking money to more affluent citizens who simply are conservation minded and/or realize they can turn trash into cash. Despite these efforts, we still generate almost twice as much waste as any other industrialized nation.

Some people with more good intentions than common sense like to cite the prehistoric American Indian as the ultimate ecologist. "They didn't waste anything," these people say. "Their entire economy was based on the buffalo. The meat they couldn't eat immediately was dried for future use. The hide was used for teepees, clothing, moccasins, quivers, knife sheaths, saddle leather, etc. Sinew was used for thread and the bones were made into needles, hide scrapers, and other tools. They even boiled the horns and shaped them into spoons."

Our self-styled ecological "experts" mean well, but they ignore basic facts. The Indians *were* wasteful, although not intentionally. It wasn't unusual for them to drive a small herd of buffalo over a cliff, then butcher the carcasses for meat and hides. What they couldn't consume or carry away with them, they left for the vultures and coyotes, or to rot in the sun. They also started prairie fires, then followed along in the wake and ate the grasshoppers which had thus been roasted. While these practices were wasteful, they were also practical from the Indians' point of view. They produced food with a minimal expenditure of energy. This was a matter of survival rather than laziness. After all, it was just as easy to kill a large buffalo as a small rabbit. In fact, it was probably easier, as there were literally millions of buffalo roaming the prairie.

Anthropologists and archeologists still speculate as to why prehistoric cliff dwellers vanished after spending several generations, or even centuries, building their fortress-like homes and establishing a highly advanced civilization. The theory most often put forward is drought, a factor which can be proven through tree ring dating. Other theories include famine due to soil and game depletion, disease, encroachment by warlike neighbors, and a combination of any or all of the above. Another theory is seldom voiced, yet it makes a great deal of sense. In some areas, at least, the Anasazi and related cultures consumed wood faster than Mother Nature could replace it. This wouldn't have been evident during the first few generations, but the end result was disastrous. When there was not enough wood for cooking or, more importantly, for winter heating, the inhabitants of a given site would have no choice but to pack a few essential belongings and move on.

Despite what some would have us believe, the cliff dwellers did generate a lot of trash. Worn-out clothing and sandals were dumped in trash heaps at the bottom of the cliffs along with broken pottery, tools, weapons and household refuse. These sites were undoubtedly nothing more than smelly eyesores to the people who created them, but they've proven to be virtual treasure troves for modern-day archeologists. Other than burial sites, they are our main sources of information regarding the everyday lifestyles of numerous vanished cultures.

Unlike prehistoric trash, which is mainly valuable only from an intellectual viewpoint, modern-day discards can be an excellent source of cash for the average American. Forget crushing soda and beer cans or throwing newspapers in the Lions Club bin in front of the neighborhood Safeway. These practices *do* help clean up the environment, but they're strictly small potatoes from an economic standpoint. Instead, concentrate on the other things people throw away. Buried among all those tons of disposable diapers, pizza cartons, grass clippings and moldy bread crusts are numerous items worth MONEY!!! Virtually every day of the year, including Sundays and holidays, people throw away carnival glass, old comic books, and the rusty pliers that came with grandpa's Model T Ford. They also throw away Uncle Oscar's North African campaign ribbon and Purple Heart, Aunt Maude's flapper dress from the 1920s, little sister's original Barbie doll and much, much more. Each of these items, plus many thousands more, is in demand by serious collectors who will gladly pay good prices for them.

In addition to collectors searching for unusual items, there are millions more who are looking for good, used, everyday items at bargain prices. No matter what the state of the economy, there is *always* a market for good, used merchandise. This is true because of the vast disparity of income groups in America. Even during the most affluent of times, there will be millions of people living in poverty. Conversely, a severe economic slump will only reduce the number of people who live well, it won't make them extinct. The vast middle class will swell during boom times, shrink when the economy slumps. In either case, the less affluent may have to live on a severely limited budget. When shopping for even the basic necessities, they might have to choose between used goods at a bargain price, or simply doing without. In other cases, people who can afford new goods prefer to buy good, serviceable used items simply because they cost less.

Beyond strictly economic or ecological motivation, there are other sound reasons for recycling. An artist or craftsperson can create attractive and even utilitarian items from scrap materials. A later chapter is devoted entirely to this aspect of recycling. Whether the artist's materials are man-made or a product of nature, he or she has the satisfaction of creating something meaningful from unwanted waste. If recycling waste into objets d'art or selling used goods seems like the long way around to making money, consider the following true-life examples:

A senior citizen with an excellent retirement income decided he wasn't satisfied with what he had, and wanted even more. He began buying and selling used goods at the local swap meet. In two years' time, he saved $54,000 from his swap meet profits alone — enough to buy himself a new motor home.

A young couple with only a couple of thousand dollars to invest literally became millionaires in one year — by buying military surplus items at government auctions, then reselling them to a select group of customers.

A starving artist in New York City started searching dumpsters for discarded items he could sell just for grocery money. One day he found a framed oil painting in a Dumpster. He wasn't familiar with the artist who had painted it, but having more nerve than sense, he immediately took the painting to a large, prestigious auction house. They auctioned the painting off for $38,000. The former starving artist took his share of the proceeds and treated himself to a luxury vacation in Paris.

An auto mechanic with a good job made over $7,000 on the side last year just buying and reselling used cars and pickups. He only sold three or four, and none of them required more than minor repairs.

A large charitable organization recently opened a thrift shop in a fairly affluent neighborhood.

During its four day grand opening, the store grossed over $13,000. It hasn't grossed less than $1,500 per day since.

A fellow who enjoys woodworking and crafts decided to try making shadow boxes from old yardsticks. He grossed over $4,000 in two days at a local craft show.

Several years ago, relatives of a lady living in Phoenix suspected that she had definitely lost her marbles. After all, who in their right mind would fill their garage with 6,000 pairs of used Levi's? Even worse, who would actually go out and *buy* that many pairs in every size imaginable? And not just *any* brand of blue jeans, but *only* genuine Levi's. What those relatives didn't know is that the lady had done her homework and had discovered a perfectly viable, and profitable, method of disposing of all those used Levi's. She now has a multi-million dollar per year business wholesaling them to clothing stores in Europe and Japan, where they're a bigger status symbol than high fashion designer clothing!

These examples may seem far-fetched, but each of them actually happened. With only a couple of exceptions, I'm personally acquainted with the individuals who made them happen. Countless other Americans are putting nice, crisp, green, spendable cash in their pockets every day of the year — simply by taking someone else's discards and selling them at a profit. Those discards aren't all used goods or broken junk, either. Some are brand new while others are unwanted products of Mother Nature. But every one of them is considered to be worthless by someone who lacks the foresight to realize their economic potential.

This book is by no means intended to be a complete guide to every potentially saleable item which might be discarded, or to its current market value. Any attempt to compile such a list would be obsolete long before it was published. It would also fill several rows of shelves at the local library. My goal is to provide an overview of the wide variety of so-called junk which can be turned into cash in *your* pocket, where to find it, and where and how to sell it. I want to help you become both a successful entrepreneur and a practicing ecologist. After all, isn't money in your pocket more desirable than an overflowing landfill?

Charlie's Clean-Out Service

I have a friend named Charlie who is a financial genius. He isn't a real estate tycoon or Wall Street manipulator. He doesn't own a limousine or a mansion in a prestigious area near the country club. In fact, Charlie is a part-time bartender, part-time actor, part-time produce delivery man and part-time swap meet vendor, and would-be screenwriter. He drives a decrepit old Ford van which looks like it came from the local junkyard, wears faded Levi's and sandals, and has long hair. He works when he wants to, takes time off when he wants to, and is in every way his own man. To look at him, one would assume he's strictly a bum, yet a couple of years ago he was interviewed by Phil Donahue on network TV.

While Charlie could make a decent living working full-time at any of the above, he prefers a variety of all of them. His mind is simply too intelligent and creative to endure the thought of doing the same thing at the same location every working day, year after year.

Of all his endeavors, his swap meet sales probably produce the most financial reward for the least expenditure of time and effort. This is true only because Charlie knows how to get his merchandise free. He doesn't steal it, he has it given to him willingly, by total strangers, simply because he isn't afraid to *think*.

It all started several years ago, when Charlie was driving past a large university campus not far from his home. It was mid-May, and he thought back to his own college years. He remembered that mid-May was the time to study for finals, look for a summer job, and get ready to go home. To most of the 40,000-plus students at the university, home was in another city or state. Charlie also knew that a large percentage of these students were from affluent families. They didn't have to live in dorms, but were able to afford apartments. They would often accumulate a lot of stuff during the school year. How much of it could they haul home when June rolled around?

Charlie's mind shifted into high gear. He switched to the right-hand lane and began searching for the visitors' parking lot. He found it, pulled into an empty space, and got out of his car. The first student he encountered was able to direct him to the office of the student newspaper.

At the newspaper office, Charlie asked the young lady at the front desk if the paper accepted classified ads from non-students. When she answered in the affirmative, he wrote out the following ad copy:

```
            FREE! FREE! FREE!
     I will clean out your apartment
   free of charge. Charlie, 876-5432.
```

When the next issue of the paper appeared the following Wednesday, Charlie's phone practically rang off the hook. He explained to each student that he didn't *clean* apartments, but would haul away anything they were unable to take home with them. Since most of them drove compact cars, that meant just about everything except their clothes and Guns & Roses albums.

For the next two weeks, Charlie was a *very* busy man. He lost track of the number of times he filled his van to capacity, hauled the stuff home and unloaded it, then went back for more. By the time he had cleaned out the last apartment, his garage, storage room and living room were overflowing with TVs, stereos, cameras, tennis rackets and kitchen utensils.

Some of the student discards were worthless and were consigned to the nearest Dumpster. A surprising number of the remainder were high ticket items in excellent condition. Since Charlie's total cash investment was a couple of dollars for the ad and less than $100 for gas, he could afford to sell these items at bargain prices and still make a very high profit.

Charlie spent the next few days sorting and categorizing his treasures, then hauled a selection to the local swap meet the following Friday afternoon. He sold enough on Friday night to recoup his entire investment, yet sales had hardly made a dent in his inventory. When he returned to the swap meet on Saturday, his first couple of sales covered his expenses for the day. Each sale beyond that point was pure profit.

Charlie continued to sell at the swap meet throughout the summer, never once having to spend a dime for merchandise. Since his only overhead was for gas and space rent, he considered $100 in sales a profitable evening's work. If his sales were less, he still didn't consider the evening a loss. There are plenty of electrical outlets at the swap meet, so he always took a TV along. If business was slow, he simply watched a movie or sports program he would have watched if he stayed home. Naturally, the TV was for sale.

In addition to his student discards, Charlie also sells new merchandise which he gets from several friends who own stores. No matter how hard merchants try to select merchandise which will sell well, they always seem to have a few items which move slowly. Sometimes they simply give these to Charlie and write them off. In other cases, they will say, "Take these and see what you can get for them. I'll split the take with you fifty-fifty." They know they will lose money on each sale, but consider it a part of doing business. In these instances, a partial return on their investment today is preferable to a potential profit sometimes in the vaguely distant future.

Charlie's lifestyle and method of earning a living may not appeal to everyone, but it suits him. Although he's only 42 years old, he owns his house free and clear. Everything else he owns is also paid for. He once told me that his net income actually exceeds his living expenses by roughly $1,000 per month. How many people who live in the right neighborhood, belong to the right clubs and are supposedly successful can say the same?

Sources of Supply

Although our main business is selling Indian arts and crafts, my wife and I also sell used paperback books at our winter swap meet location. Most of our customers are upper middle class retirees who have plenty of time to read. "Where do you get your books?" they often ask. Our stock answer is evasive but honest. "All over," we tell them.

If they press further, we proceed to tell them that we buy books all over the state, which is true. Of course, our out-of-town purchases are usually made while traveling to and from the Indian reservation for new merchandise, but that answer effectively stops customers from trying to find our sources and buying direct.

We got into the swap meet business in an indirect way, and have gone full circle from selling our own household goods, to strictly new merchandise, to a combination of the two types, but it can work if done properly.

When I lost my job in the winter of 1985, we cleaned out our rented, garage-size storage room and hauled the stuff to the local swap meet. Sales were brisk the first two or three weekends, then began dropping off since the most desirable items had already been sold.

As we looked around us, we realized that a number of vendors were regular dealers who sold *new* merchandise every weekend. Several seemed to be doing very well at it. We looked at our dwindling supply of household goods and said, "Well, if I don't find a job soon, we can always sell at the swap meet." While that option certainly wasn't our first choice, it ultimately became the only choice.

I never did find a regular job, but we've been making a living in the swap meet business for several years.

With our stock of used household goods almost exhausted, we invested every cent we could spare in Indian arts and crafts. Business was good the first season, and we spent most of the winter constantly expanding our inventory. The second year was a real eye-opener. It didn't take us long to discover that what sold extremely well one year might not be popular the next. In the ensuing years, we constantly looked for and found, new sources of supply. This enabled us to actually increase our sales each year for several years.

When the economy took a drastic turn for the worse a couple of years ago, our sales did likewise. We knew there was always a demand for good used items, especially in hard times. Given the demographics of our customer base, a used paperback setup was the logical choice to boost our sagging sales. Just how well this worked, and why, will be covered extensively in a later chapter. Suffice to say that we soon found ourselves scrambling for new sources of supply. The stock we had expected to last most of the winter was nearly depleted after only three or four weekends' sales!

With few exceptions, our major sources for books are also good sources of supply for virtually any type of common used goods. They are by no means the only sources, but they're at least a starting point.

Home

Virtually everyone, unless they're a vagabond, manages to accumulate a lot of unwanted stuff over the years. It can be anything from duplicate wedding gifts to specialized hobby or sports items that were used regularly a few years ago, but now gather dust in a corner of the garage. Start by going through all the storage areas of your own home. You will be amazed at the things you've forgotten you have. A good rule of thumb is: "If I didn't even remember I had it, I don't need it." Any item that fits into the category is a prime candidate to be sold. So you only get $25 for that set of golf clubs worth $150. If you haven't used them in the last five years, isn't that $25 in your pocket a lot more beneficial? Be realistic as to pricing, what is actually saleable, and what isn't. Throw out anything that is just plain junk. Too many people at yard sales and swap meets try to sell items that should simply be deposited in the nearest Dumpster.

Friends & Neighbors

Put the word out among your friends and neighbors that you're looking for good used items to sell. After all, they accumulate a lot of stuff, too. In some cases, they will gladly give you their unwanted items. In others, they may want to make a little money themselves. If the price is right, go ahead and buy, but remember that you have to be able to resell those items at a profit.

If you specialize in a certain type of item and have friends whose judgment you can trust, let them do some scouting for you. Last year a friend of ours ran across what he thought was a real deal on paperback books. He bought them — all 11 boxes full! Unfortunately, he made the mistake of assuming that any old paperback would automatically sell. We paid him what he had invested in them, then began sorting. Six full boxes of cheap romances in poor condition immediately went into the nearest Dumpster. Out of the remaining five boxes, approximately 20 percent of the books were the type we needed. The remainder were potentially saleable in a large used book store, but not to our clientele. We simply cleaned those books up and hauled them off to trade. What the first store didn't want, we took to yet another book store, repeating the process until we only had a few left which no one wanted. These we simply threw away.

While the above process might seem time-consuming and wasteful, it was necessary. From the original 11 boxes of paperbacks, we wound up with about three boxes of really prime titles. Any one of those titles had at least a 50-50 chance of selling the following weekend. The stuff we traded *might* have sold, but there was also a chance we would still have most of it a year later. When I totaled up the value of the books we had left, the potential net profit was far greater than we had dared hope.

Yard Sales

Yard sales, also known as garage sales, are a uniquely American institution, probably because so many Americans have yards and garages. They're also an excellent source of goods which can be recycled into money in your pocket. I know one fellow who alternates weekends buying at yard sales, then reselling his purchases at the swap meet the following weekend. He hasn't worked a regular job for several years simply because he can't afford to! He makes more money in four days of selling each month than he could make in four weeks of working.

Yard sales aren't difficult to find. Simply pick up the classified ads of the local newspaper and start reading. Larger newspapers will even have them categorized by the areas of the city. Most ads will contain at least a partial listing of items being offered for sale. Typical ads will read something like this:

MULTI-FAMILY YARD SALE
Baby clothes, books, refrigerator, aquarium, outboard motor, tools, etc.
Sat., 9 'til it gets hot.
1234 Cypress Lane.

or

GLENWOOD AREA
Sat. only, 7 'til 3. Everything must go.
Lots of goodies. 5678 W. Belmont Ave.
234-5678.

If you don't see anything in the ad you want, but there is a phone number, call and ask what they have that isn't listed. Since classified ads are sold by the line, the person placing the ad will usually keep it short and to the point. They list only a small sampling of the items they intend to sell. Even if several phone calls produce negative results, the time isn't wasted. You will know ahead of time which sales *not* to attend, thus saving both time and gas on Saturday morning.

Obviously, the most promising sales are the ones to visit first. Try to arrive early for the best selection, but not too early. If an ad states the sale begins at 7:00 a.m., don't show up before dawn. The people having the sale will probably still be in bed.

Some yard salers will have the price of each item marked. You will have to ask others for prices. Don't be persuaded to buy something just because it's cheap. Ask yourself how much you could realistically expect to get for it, and how quickly. After all, your objective is to make money, not just get rid of things. While many yard sale prices are negotiable, this isn't always true. A person may feel that if they can't get a certain price for an item, they will simply keep it. In other cases, they may be firm at the start of the sale, but willing to negotiate at the end of the day. If they turn down your offer in the morning, go back in the afternoon, or close to whatever time the sale is to end. This method is a calculated risk, as the items you want may be gone, but they might also still be there. At that point, the seller may be more than willing to accept your offer.

It's often possible to get a better price when buying in quantity. This applies whether buying just one type of item or virtually everything they have for sale. Of course, there are right and wrong ways to go about this. "I'll give you twenty dollars for all those stuffed animals" might or might not work on a yard saler. It definitely *won't* work on a professional swap meet vendor. No approach will turn them off quicker!

A far better approach is to use one of the following phrases: "Could you do any better on these prices if I took all the baby clothes?", or "What's the least you'll take for the entire lot?" When the latter approach is accompanied by the sight of a couple of $100 bills in your hand, it can become *very* tempting for the seller. No one likes to see those big bills slip away from their imminent grasp.

Only time and practice will help you decide which approach works best for you, and under what circumstances. Some people with a brash yet friendly manner can get away with a cruder approach than others. Of course, it never hurts to smile, no matter what line you use. Even if your offer is ridiculously low, the seller will undoubtedly turn you down with a smile. That will put you both in better humor than you were before.

Classified Ads

In addition to yard sales, newspaper classifieds offer a virtual treasure trove of merchandise for the recycling entrepreneur. The Sunday classified section is the largest of the entire week, hence the most productive. Simply turn to the appropriate listing (furniture, jewelry, antiques, sporting goods, computers, etc.) and start working your way down the list. You can bet most large antique dealers read the classifieds regularly, but they aren't the only ones. I used to work for a newspaper publisher who also owned an auto dealership. He had a distinct advantage over his competition. He would simply walk into the composing room and read the car ads on the page paste ups. Needless to say, most of the better cars were sold before the newspaper ever hit the stands.

Auctions

There are auctions, and then there are auctions. At one end of the scale are the weekly neighborhood auctions. These are often held in a run-down warehouse or the parking lot of a defunct gas station or convenience market. At the other end of the scale are the ultra-exclusive variety such as Sotheby's. Some of the latter are strictly for the highest of the high rollers. Even your typical, everyday Texas oil tycoon might as well pick up his marbles and go home before the bidding starts. As an example, an oil painting by Van Gogh recently sold to a Japanese consortium for $84,000,000 at one such auction. Obviously, they weren't buying to resell at that kind of price!

A number of swap meet vendors regularly attend the aforementioned neighborhood auctions. One fellow told me he usually pays $2 to $3 for a box of mixed items. He and his wife then sort out the china and glassware they want and sell it at the swap meet the following weekend. The remainder goes back to the auction the next week. More than once, the stock they turned back in netted him more than he paid for the entire lot the week before! Such profitable deals aren't that common, but they do happen. If it happened to him, it can happen to you!

An often overlooked source of merchandise is storage unit auctions. The larger storage companies regularly auction off the contents of lockers to recoup unpaid back rent. Some part-time swap meet vendors obtain virtually *all* their merchandise in this manner. They often have no idea what they're bidding on, as it's just a specific lot of sealed boxes. It's easy to tell when another vendor has bought out a storage unit. Just ask what's in the un-opened boxes, They will answer, "I don't know." The more canny of these vendors will open the boxes as soon as they take possession of them. Quite often, they will make back their entire investment, plus a profit, simply by selling specific items to other bidders.

Another excellent source of merchandise is bank-ruptcy auctions. These are usually listed in the local newspaper and aren't necessarily the result of Joe Blow living beyond his means. All types of businesses go bank-rupt each year. Items going on the auction block will de-pend on the type of business, but may include vehicles, machinery, office equipment, store fixtures and inven-tory. In the case of the latter, the items will generally be brand new. It may be possible to bid on individual lots, but in many cases you will have to bid on the entire in-ventory. Don't be discouraged if this is the case. The en-tire lot may go so cheaply that it can be resold profitably at mere pennies on the dollar of its original *wholesale* value. As an example, several years ago my wife bought a *large* grocery bag full of vitamins and homeopathic remedies from a fellow who had purchased the inventory of a bankrupt health food store. All the boxes and bottles were still sealed and bore the store's original price tags. If we had paid the store's prices for all those goodies, it would have cost us well over $200. As it was, the tab came to $22. We got a bargain, and the other vendor *still* made a decent profit.

Swap Meets

Believe it or not, a large number of professional swap meet vendors buy their used goods from other vendors at the same swap meet. As with yard sales, the trick is to get there early. One couple I know has an excellent routine worked out. They arrive at their assigned spot shortly before the sun comes up. While he sets up their tables and lays out the merchandise, she walks around looking for anything that appeals to her. She has a two-wheeled shopping cart and simply puts her purchases in it as she goes. This usually takes less than an hour. By the time the first real influx of customers arrives, she has the morning's purchases priced and on display.

Other vendors prefer to walk around and look for a yard saler who has a number of appealing items, but not too many. They will make a blanket offer for the entire lot. Quite often, the seller will accept the offer and be long gone by the time the buyer adds his purchases to his own wares.

Some swap meets run double sessions. In other words, the first session runs from early morning until mid-afternoon, then the second runs into the evening hours. A canny vendor can do well buying just as the first session ends and the second begins. People who have worked the first will be anxious to go home. Those who have just arrived will often welcome a quick sale, especially if it involves everything they have. They know they can be long gone before the swap meet staff comes around to collect the space rent.

My favorite story concerning buying and selling at a double session swap meet will serve to illustrate just how profitable this can be. A regular vendor waited until the first session was almost over, then approached the young man who was set up next to her. He wore nothing but cut-offs and shoes, and was now paying for his hours in the sun with a bad sunburn. "I'll give your $5 for everything you have left," she said. Despite her "I'll give you" approach, the young man quickly replied, "Sold!" Within minutes, he was on his way home. The lucky buyer shifted her purchases into her own space, then awaited the first customer. That night, she sold several of those items for a total of $85, and still had a few left.

Just as it pays to start buying early, it also pays to walk through the swap meet after the selling session is over. Some yard salers don't want to take *anything* home, and will leave perfectly good items just sitting where they unloaded them. In other cases, they will gladly give you their leftovers. I still remember asking a guy set up across from us how much he wanted for a three-way desk lamp at the end of one session. "Take it, it's yours," he replied. Such luck doesn't happen all the time, but it does happen. I've seen people drive off and leave perfectly good fishing poles, folding chairs, sofas, and the like on more than one occasion.

Thrift Shops

Many used goods dealers, including the Coopers, rely heavily on thrift shops for much of their merchandise. These shops often have a good selection of items in excellent condition. The bad news is that they know dealers regularly buy from them, so their prices are often too high to enable you to resell at a profit.

My wife and I laugh, and none too merrily, at how the prices of paperbacks fluctuate from summer to winter in our area. This is because winter visitors outnumber permanent residents by at least two to one, hence there is a greater demand in the winter. Paperbacks may sell for 10 cents each in the summer, or at the most three for $1. In October, the price jumps to 50 cents for run-of-the-mill titles and as much as $2 for the most popular titles and authors. Sometime between the middle of April and the first of May, the prices go back down. Needless to say, we try to buy from some of these shops only in the summer, or on half-price days. Half-price day will vary from shop to shop, but it's usually every Monday or the first and third Wednesday of the month.

It doesn't take long before the more alert thrift shop employees begin to recognize those individuals who buy only certain types of merchandise, and in quantity. Don't try to hide the fact that you're a dealer, it can actually work to your advantage. Let the manager or a key employee know you are interested in certain items in good condition. Depending on store policy, they may be able to save these items for you. In some cases, they will even be willing to call you when a particularly good selection arrives in the stock room. The manager of one shop knows my wife will be in every Monday afternoon, so she purposely delays stocking the paperback shelves until late in the day. She also saves certain popular authors and titles, knowing my wife will take every copy she has. The arrangement is advantageous to both of us. We get the books we need, and the store manager has less work to do pricing and stocking. Since we pay the going rate (on half-price day, naturally), the store makes the same amount of money either way.

Some thrift shops consistently seem to have a good selection of certain types of merchandise, a poor selection of others. This disparity may reflect the demographics of a store's clientele, but not always. In one exceptional case, my wife could never understand why a certain store always had a fair number of new paperbacks on hand, but never any of the most desirable categories and titles. When she mentioned it to the manager, he told her the reason. "There are three ladies who live nearby who sell books at the Linda Vista swap meet," he explained. "They're friends, and they sell different types of books to avoid competing with each other. One sells romance, another sells Westerns and historicals, and the third sells mysteries and major novels. They stock our shelves on a volunteer basis three times a day." No wonder the shelves were always barren of good titles. They never made it that far!

Other Sources

In addition to the above-mentioned, fairly common sources, there are other specialized sources which should be mentioned. Antique and rare book dealers frequently attend estate sales and auctions. These can be profitable sources, unless they're run by professionals. In that case, many items may be priced at or above full market value. A recent estate sale in our neighborhood proved to be a real eye-opener. Several people who were obviously dealers walked in, looked around, and walked out empty-handed. Conversely, we watched a handful of bargain hunters pay $10 or more for used items that go begging at the swap meet for $3.

Occasionally, construction sites can be a lucrative source, and I don't mean in the steal of the night. On larger projects, contractors generally order an average of materials to allow for damage, mistakes, etc. When the job is finished, they have to do something with the left-overs. They don't want to go to the expense of loading them up and hauling them back to the storage yard. One fellow I know approached the contractor on a small shopping center site and inquired what he would take for the leftover rebar. "What'll you give me?" the contractor asked. My friend then explained he only had $20 in his wallet. "Sold!" the contractor exclaimed. "Back your pickup up to the stack and we'll help you load her." My friend hauled almost a ton of rebar home and used it to reinforce the roof on his new fallout shelter.

Building *de*struction sites also offer possibilities for good saleable items. Used, well-weathered barn wood is in constant demand for picture frames. In some areas of the country, certain types of used bricks are also in de-mand. Ditto with the doors that contained stained glass windows which were popular around the turn of the century. Of course, be sure to obtain permission from the property owner or demolition crew before removing anything from such a site. They may want a small recom-pense for what you haul away, but they may also just be happy to get rid of it.

Dumpster Diving For Fun & Profit

Recently I rediscovered Dumpster diving. My previous experience at it had been limited to looking for large packing boxes for moving. Not exactly a thrilling pastime, but sometimes a necessary one.

Imagine my surprise when I opened the resident Dumpster next to our driveway a few days ago and discovered a nice, shiny blue bicycle. Well, at least most of it was shiny, and at a casual glance it appeared to be in perfectly serviceable condition.

Since I know a fellow who repairs bicycles, then sells them at the local swap meet, I immediately rushed to the phone and gave him a call. Ordinarily, there wouldn't have been any hurry, but it was trash pickup day. My friend arrived within a few minutes, and together we fished the bike out of the Dumpster. Closer inspection revealed that the seat was torn and the chain missing. All in all, the bike was repairable, therefore saleable.

Although our Dumpster diving reinforced the fact that the practice can be profitable, we had by no means made a startling discovery. Actually, a number of otherwise perfectly normal people dive on a regular basis. One professional autograph dealer even dives behind movie stars' homes. No, they don't throw away autographed photos, old Oscars or anything like that. They do, however, throw away canceled checks, notes to the maid, grocery lists, etc. This dealer knows that anything bearing their signatures or verifiable handwriting is saleable. As an example, a check that Marilyn Monroe signed just a few days before her death was recently sold at auction for $15,000. That's more than 1,000 times the amount for which it was written! Incidentally, many movie stars regularly write checks for very small amounts, knowing full well the check will never be cashed. Their signature is worth more than the cash value of the check!

A garbage collector in Aspen, Colorado, was recently quoted as saying he furnished his entire house from Dumpsters. He even found a perfectly good motor scooter next to a Dumpster along his route. The only thing wrong with it was a torn seat. It seems many people in wealthy neighborhoods believe it's beneath their dignity to donate their discards to charities. They simply throw the stuff away!

Until recently, Dumpster diving has been a closely guarded secret, akin to illegitimate birth or admitting that your favorite uncle was once a member of the Communist Party, or a Nazi spy. It has only recently gained publicity as an ever-growing national sport. Instead of coming out of the closet, Dumpster divers are now coming out of the garbage. Their ranks include construction workers, pediatricians, engineers, interior decorators — you name it! Contrary to popular belief, it isn't just the homeless who dive. In fact, a large percentage of divers have decent jobs and don't really *need* to do it, except psychologically. "It's addictive," they say, "kind of like being a prospector who has already struck it rich, but still keeps looking for the Mother Lode."

How many people have you seen in front of supermarkets lately with HOMELESS VIETNAM VET, WILL WORK FOR FOOD signs in their hands? Probably quite a few. How much edible food is in the Dumpster behind the supermarket? Depending on the time of day, it might be enough to feed one of those bums for a week. If there is good food to be had just a few feet away, why don't the homeless dive? The answer is simple. Why *work* to get mere food out of a Dumpster when they can con some poor sucker into handing them actual money? They can then spend it on food, booze, drugs or whatever else they want. Don't waste your sympathy on these bums; many are a lot better off than you might think. Not too long ago, a news team from one of the major TV networks interviewed a "homeless" panhandler in New York City. The guy readily admitted that he frequently grosses as much as $3,000 per week begging on street corners. He is also in the habit of renting a chauffeured limousine for monthly trips to Atlantic City, where he receives the red carpet treatment provided only to high rollers. And, of course, that $3,000 per week is all tax-free.

But this book is about making money from other people's discards, not cutting your food bill by diving, or making a fortune as a panhandler. Forget the supermarket Dumpsters unless you're hungry. Concentrate on looking for goodies you can sell or trade for something that is saleable.

There are, of course, certain guidelines for Dumpster diving. If possible, dive in a medium-sized city. The competition will be less fierce, as the homeless generally congregate in large metropolitan areas. Of course, diving will be much more lucrative in an affluent neighborhood than in the local ghetto. Not only will the competition be less, but your "haul" will undoubtedly be better. Diving should also be best right after dark, as people tend to throw things away in the late afternoon and early evening.

When preparing to dive, dress appropriately. Durable, nondescript, yet presentable clothing is best. It's perfectly okay to look like you might be having a little trouble making ends meet. Just don't look like a homeless wino. Basically, the less conspicuous you are, the better. If no one notices you, they won't call the cops. Avoid *any* clothing that makes you look like a member of the so-called "lunatic fringe." Black leather jackets, punk haircuts, cammies or long hair and beards automatically make many people suspicious, even if there is no reason to be. "Different" simply arouses their latent Sheriff Bubba mentality.

Carry a dive stick (a piece of 1 x 2 or an old broom handle will do) to pull stuff toward you. It seems to be one of Murphy's laws that the most desirable items in any given Dumpster are also the least accessible. For safety's sake, avoid actually climbing into the Dumpster if at all possible. Thick-soled shoes will protect your feet from broken glass, both within and outside the Dumpster. Always keep one hand on the Dumpster lid to keep it from falling on you. Avoid climbing or reaching into Dumpsters that are off balance. If you have to lean against the rim, use a piece of cardboard as a cushion. Not only will it be more comfortable, but it will keep your clothes clean as well.

When working a regular Dumpster route in your car or pickup, always carry a few good, heavy, empty boxes with you. They're great for holding smaller Dumpster treasures, but they also serve another practical purpose. If someone in authority (the cops, a store employee, etc.)

should challenge you, the boxes can add credibility to a good cover story. "Gee, I didn't mean to do anything wrong," you can say. "I was just looking for some good, sturdy boxes to house my record collection (or for moving, etc.)." Say as little as possible, just enough to cover a graceful retreat. After all, there is always another Dumpster just down the street.

While the above covers the basics of Dumpster diving, it is by no means all-inclusive. For a complete course in the subject, including postgraduate work, read *The Art & Science Of Dumpster Diving* by John Hoffman (Loompanics Unlimited, 1993). It's written by a past master of the art, a man who has been doing it almost his entire life. The book is an irreverent but relevant, highly entertaining read, and is probably the most practical survival guide ever written for city dwellers.

If Dumpster diving isn't your forte, don't despair. There are still numerous other sources of good, saleable used merchandise.

INCISORAUS
FEROCIOUS
400,000,000 B.C.

Clean It! Paint It! Fix It!

Several months ago, I went shopping for a cast iron skillet at the swap meet. One vendor had several that were just the right size, but I never got beyond looking at the first one. The mere sight of the dried food stuck to it grossed me out — and cost that vendor a sale. Even though the price was right, only 50 cents, I refused to pay even that paltry sum for an item in such deplorable condition. As I recall, the other skillets were just about as dirty, but I only glanced at them as I went down the aisle.

The saddest part of all is that the vendor wasn't a yard saler, but a so-called professional who has been selling in the same location for more years than I can count. How many other sales has he lost over the years simply because he was too lazy to clean his merchandise? There is no way to calculate it, but I would bet the dollar amount is considerable.

By contrast, another vendor I know who sells nothing but used goods always has a presentable display. His merchandise is sometimes dusty, which is understandable at any outdoor location, but it's *never* just plain rusty, cracked, broken or downright dirty. When I needed a toaster oven several years ago, I didn't hesitate a minute to buy one from him. It was clean, and he guarantees all his small appliances. "If it doesn't work, bring it back," he tells his customers. Needless to say, he does a good business.

Frankly, I'm appalled at the number of used goods vendors, yard salers and pros alike, who haul worthless junk to the swap meet and expect to sell it. What's even worse, they will load the stuff back into their car or pickup at the end of the day, then unload it again the next time they go out to sell. They would be further ahead just throwing it away, as we did the six boxes of unsaleable paperbacks mentioned in the Sources of Supply chapter.

One paperback dealer I know has spent several seasons loading and unloading the same boxes of cheap romances. Some have missing covers while others have been wet. He wonders why he can't sell them, even at eight for $1. Frankly, he would be further ahead selling them for scrap paper. He might at least get enough out of them to pay for gas he would use hauling them to the recycling station.

Even when a vendor has some desirable items, they probably won't sell if they're mixed in with broken lamps, rusty tools and stained clothing. While some customers *will* take the time to rummage through a variety of junk looking for treasures, others are influenced by their first impression. "There's nothing worthwhile here," they say after a quick glance, then walk away.

Some items which are virtually unsaleable "as-is" could be made appealing, and at a higher price, with just a little effort. The skillet I turned down is a perfect example. If the vendor had just spent a few minutes cleaning it up, I would gladly have paid $3 for it. As it is, he's probably still trying to sell it for 50 cents.

Rusty tools *can* be cleaned up. They may not look brand new, but they will at least be presentable. Minor scratches on wooden furniture can usually be masked with a good grade of furniture polish. Wrought iron book ends or candlesticks which are dirt-encrusted and rusty are comparatively easy to clean. Simply scrape off the worst of the dirt and rust, then turn the hose on them. After letting them dry in the sun (or drying them with a hair dryer), simply spray them with a can of flat black enamel. They will look almost new.

When cleaning or repairing used goods, weigh the time and cost involved against the potential selling price. It isn't worth spending two hours trying to get every speck of mud out of a pair of tennis shoes that *might* bring $1. It *is* worth spending $10 for parts and investing an hour's time in a bicycle that might sell for $50 or more, especially if you fished it out of a Dumpster. The bottom line is: If it can't be exhibited in presentable condition, don't waste your time trying to sell it.

Some Tips On Merchandising

The very first time we set up to sell used goods at a swap meet, another vendor asked my wife how many years we had been in the business. He was shocked to learn we were rank amateurs, just selling off our surplus household goods.

Looking back on the experience, I can well understand why he was fooled. We didn't just throw everything out on the ground, and with good reason. The few patches of ground that didn't have snow on them were muddy. We didn't have tarps to lay on the ground, so we borrowed folding picnic tables from a couple of neighbors and interspersed them with our own two card tables. That wasn't enough for my wife. She raided the linen closet and used clean white sheets for table covers. Then she proceeded to arrange everything neatly on the tables. She also bought a package of Avery labels and priced each item individually. In short, our jerry-rigged setup looked like a professional display. Not only did it keep our merchandise dry, it also raised it to waist level where customers could see it better — and could read the prices without having to ask.

Needless to say, we were the success story of the day. Of course, that wasn't hard to do under the circumstances. That particular swap meet was held in the parking lot of the corner saloon in a small country town. No one knew when a stray cow might literally wander down the single aisle between vendors. There was only space for 10 to 15 vendors so competition was minimal.

At the end of the day, we had grossed over $400, just selling so-called "junk." Not only did that day's sales pay our groceries for the next few weeks, it also taught us a valuable lesson. The more effective a display, the better sales will normally be.

A display of used goods doesn't have to, and probably shouldn't, look like the front window of Macy's. It *should*, however, have as much eye appeal as possible. My wife is no artist, but she can put together an attractive display even when she seemingly has nothing to work with. Although I'm a better than average artist, I have about as much display ability as a giraffe. My theory is to just get the stuff out on the tables in some semblance of order so customers can see it. While my way saves time and energy, I'll have to admit hers is probably best. After all, I don't like to see stuff all jumbled together when I go bargain hunting. Anyone who has ever seen my office might not believe I like things in an orderly manner, but it's true. However, we're talking about merchandising here, not a picture layout in *Architectural Digest*.

First and foremost, potential customers need to be able to see the merchandise. If at all possible, lay it out on tables, don't just throw it on the ground. I know one swap meet where customers from low-income families will rummage through cardboard boxes full of baby clothes, but it's the exception. I'm sure those poor, tired ladies hauling three snot-nosed, whining brats behind them and with yet another on its way would much rather sort through stacks of clothing at waist level. Using tables will also ease your own burden. Except for very large items, it's much easier to load and unload from waist height instead of ground level.

Group items according to category. Don't mix adult-size shoes with baby clothes, old sports equipment with kitchen equipment, etc. Remember, however, there is a difference between a hodgepodge and deliberate separation of the same type of merchandise into two or more separate groups. Let's assume you sell both men's and women's clothing. You also sell kitchen utensils and tools. It's perfectly acceptable to put the women's clothing and kitchen utensils in one section, the men's clothing and tools in another. In other words, group merchandise according to customer appeal rather than category. It's know as creative misfiling.

The best example of working on the basis of customer appeal was demonstrated by a fellow I saw at the state fair several years ago. He sold nothing but knives and earrings. He obviously hadn't chosen that combination by accident, but concentrated on both male and female customer appeal. A man won't mind if his wife wants to stop and look at earrings if he can look at knives at the same time, and vice versa.

Generally speaking, the greater the variety of merchandise the better your sales potential. Don't get too carried away with variety, however, or you are right back to having hodgepodge.

Some vendors prefer to specialize in one or two particular types of merchandise. With the right selection, they can do extremely well. I especially remember one fellow who had nothing but cast iron skillets and Dutch ovens. His skillets ranged in size from just large enough to fry an egg to one that looked like it could cook enough breakfast to feed a whole troop of Boy Scouts. In contrast to the dirty skillet described in the last chapter, Big Tiny's skillets were all spotlessly clean.

One family I know works together, but each member has his or her own specialty, with which they are thoroughly familiar. The husband sells video movies and camping gear, while the wife handles baby clothes. The eldest daughter specializes in china and glassware. Her kid sister hustles stuffed animals, and what a hustler she is! If I had a kid like that, I could send her to the swap meet while I stayed home and counted the money!

Many people make a habit of visiting their local swap meet virtually every weekend, weather permitting. While some are actually shopping, others just like to browse or walk around in crowds. They quickly become bored with seeing the same old thing week after week. Anything that will attract attention is a definite plus. If you are even a halfway decent musician, by all means play your harmonica, fiddle or guitar. But have mercy on your fellow vendors. *Don't* set up a 400-watt amplifier and blast everyone with hard rock from your electric guitar. It might be what you like, but a lot of people hate rock and will run in the opposite direction. Early rock and roll, as in Elvis and Jerry Lee Lewis, or country music are safe compromises. A little too tame for the youngsters, maybe a little too wild for the geriatric set, but at least bearable for almost anyone. Keep the volume low so the vendor next to you won't have trouble conversing with customers. Of course, if a customer stops at your setup, stop playing long enough to wait on them.

Virtually any type of entertainment will attract potential customers, whether it's of professional caliber or not.

If there is a puppet among your merchandise, play with it. A six-foot five linebacker type would look like an idiot hugging a large stuffed animal, but his petite wife or ten-year-old daughter will attract smiles rather than strange looks.

One fellow I know doesn't sell any merchandise at all, but he certainly attracts attention and collects a lot of money. He simply takes a pet monkey to the swap meet and erects a sign reading "Give The Monkey A Quarter And He'll Shake Your Hand." People actually stand in line to hand the monkey quarters. He shakes their hand, tips his hat, and sticks his tongue out at them. For $3, the man will take a color Polaroid picture of customers with the monkey.

Another fellow bought a very nice, used telescope at the swap meet and quickly turned a profit on it *without* selling. The swap meet was open that night and there was a full moon. He simply rented an empty space, erected the telescope, and quickly lettered a sign that read "Look At The Moon: 50¢." Like the fellow with the monkey, he quickly attracted a crowd that was willing to pay 50 cents for a couple of minutes' entertainment.

Yet another enterprising fellow devised a unique way to turn what might have been a poor selling day into a financial success. Among the items he was trying to sell were some mismatched plates, saucers, Tupperware lids and poster board. No one was seriously looking at them, so he went down the aisle and bought several cans of spray paint in various colors. Using his mismatched dishware as circular templates, he laid his poster board on the ground and began spray-painting it to resemble pictures of various planets in space. While he didn't sell a great many of them, he did sell enough to pay for his spray paint plus a small profit. From then on, whenever he went to the swap meet to sell, he augmented his sales with his outer space Picasso act.

One yard saler who has turned semi-pro has a sales gimmick that is a lot of work, but he claims it increases his sales. After unloading his pickup, he will start loading it up again. He will get it about half loaded, then unload it again. His theory is that people who think he has just arrived believe they will get first choice. Those who think he is leaving rush over to get a bargain before he goes home.

If you have an unusual item and have no idea what it might be, put it on display anyway. Someone, somewhere, *will* know. In the meantime, simply tell customers, "I don't know what it is, but it's kid of neat, so I figure somebody will buy it." While ignorance of your merchandise is generally a poor idea, in this case it's calculated ignorance. You are using the item to attract attention, which brings people to your table.

A friend of mine lives in a rural area which has a heavy concentration of hunters, survivalists and other outdoor types. He puts his hunting rifle at the forefront of his merchandise. "I don't really want to sell it, but it brings a lot of people over, and I figure they'll buy something else," he explains.

Despite admonitions elsewhere to keep merchandise clean, I realize it isn't always possible. Last year, my wife and I worked a market we had never tried before. We were unaware of the direction of the prevailing wind, and set up in what looked like a good spot. For the next three days, we fumed with frustration as the afternoon winds turned our setup into a virtual dust bowl. We would dust everything at least twice a day, but to no avail. Finally, we began telling customers, "The merchandise was clean when we came, but we guarantee it's dusty now. In fact, we'll even give you a written guarantee and sign it in blood." The line didn't help sell much merchandise, but it did get quite a few laughs.

Swap Meet Survival

In the preceding chapters, I have consistently used swap meets and swap meet vendors as examples for selling used goods. There are several reasons for this. First and foremost, it's the logical place to sell used goods in volume. Second, my wife and I have had over eight years' full-time experience in the business, selling both new and used goods. Third, many people who are looking for used goods will automatically shop the local swap meet first. These people are the backbone of the swap meet economy. Despite the proliferation of thrift shops in recent years, this situation isn't likely to change in the foreseeable future.

For those unfamiliar with them, swap meets are generally large, open-air markets where a number of vendors gather to sell both new and used goods. The term swap meet is most common in California, Arizona and Nevada. People in other states call them flea markets, a term which I thoroughly hate. I mean, who wants to go out and buy fleas? You can get plenty off the nearest stray dog or cat. Of course, neither term is truly descriptive. Very little swapping takes place at swap meets.

In some areas of the country, indoor swap meets prevail due to inclement weather. In these areas, outdoor swap meets generally have at least some covered selling spaces. Where good weather prevails, outdoor swap meets are most common. My wife and I live in the Sun Belt, so we almost always work outdoors. In fact, we have never worked an indoor swap meet in our lives. The concept was introduced to our area several years ago, with very limited success. The first indoor swap meet barely lasted two years, and with good reason. The space rent was too high and foot traffic was too low. These two problems continue to plague indoor swap meets in our area and will probably prevent them from ever becoming popular — or successful.

When selling used goods, swap meets offer several distinct advantages over other marketplaces. Chief among these are:

1. *Low overhead.* The only expense involved is space rent and gas to get to and from the swap meet. If you don't take in a lot of money on a given day or weekend, you probably also won't have lost any. In contrast, imagine leasing a storefront at $600 per month (cheap), then only grossing $300 per month. It *has* happened!

2. *Numerous locations.* Depending on population density, there may be anywhere from one to a dozen swap meets within a reasonable driving distance of your home. They are *not* all the same! One might have a customer base of young, low-income families. Used goods will sell well there. Another, five miles away, may be frequented mainly by middle-class professionals and retirees. Most vendors will probably sell new goods. Yet another nearby swap meet might attract a cross-section of all racial and ethnic types, economic classes and age levels. What sells extremely well at the first swap meet might sell very poorly at the second, about equally well, a little better or a little worse at the third. Sales of particular items will even

vary in the same market from day to day or from one weekend to the next.

3. *Built-in customer base.* Many of the larger swap meets attract thousands of people each weekend. While some come mainly to browse or just walk around and enjoy the crowded atmosphere, a great many will be serious shoppers. Naturally, not everyone will be interested in what *you* have, but some will.

4. *Flexibility.* Most swap meets rent selling space by the day or by the weekend. If you don't do well at Fat Eddie's Swap Meet, you can always try Pacific Boulevard Stop and Swap next weekend. Some of the larger swap meets *do* offer leases or contract agreements. These ensure that a vendor will be able to set up in a particular spot every weekend. Usually, you will pay in advance for this privilege. Some swap meets require contract vendors to pay one week in advance while others have a monthly fee payable on the last Sunday of the preceding month. Some smaller swap meets have no formal contract agreement, but the owner or manager will save a particular space for a regular vendor who requests it. If you plan to sell every weekend and find that you consistently do well at a particular swap meet, I strongly recommend signing a contract.

The only disadvantage is that swap meet managers often require contract vendors to have a sales tax license. It isn't necessarily their idea, but may be required by law or bureaucratic edict. I know one city which can fine the swap meet owner and vendor *each* up to $2,500 if they find a regular vendor who doesn't have a city license. And most people think the Nazis who survived World War Two all fled to Argentina! There is little you can do about such regulations except comply, then spend as much time as you want cussing the @#&%@# bureaucrats from city hall all the way back to Washington. Don't worry about offending a particular lawmaker or bureaucrat. A very high percentage of them deserve it.

Selling at swap meets can be a pleasant experience, a traumatic nightmare, or anything in-between. This is especially true if the experience is entirely new. By simply following the Boy Scout motto of "Be Prepared," however, a lot of potentially unpleasant situations can be avoided. There are certain guidelines which, if followed, should greatly increase your personal comfort, safety, and chances of financial success.

First and foremost, *do your homework!* Don't load the car on Saturday morning and drive down to Fat Eddie's only to discover it's open only on Wednesday and Sunday. Most swap meets are listed in the Yellow Pages, although the heading may be for flea markets. Call ahead. You may get a recording which merely states, "Thank you for calling Fat Eddie's Swap Meet. Hours are seven to five each Wednesday and Sunday. Spaces measure twelve by twenty feet and cost five dollars each. Clean rest rooms and a snack bar are provided for your shopping and selling convenience." That might not seem like a lot of information, but it at least covers the basics.

If a live person answers the phone, ask some of the questions on the following list, in addition to obtaining the information given above. It may seem like a lot of questions, but from the reasons listed in parentheses, it should be obvious that none is frivolous. The answer given to any one of them might determine whether you decide to try or reject a specific swap meet.

- Approximately how many customers attend each weekend?
- How many selling spaces are there? (Swap meets vary greatly in size, and any given one might be too large or too small to be lucrative for you.)
- What specific types of merchandise are prohibited, if any? (Some swap meets permit the sale of anything that is legal. Others prohibit the sale of certain items such as firearms, explosive devices [including snap caps], pornographic material, etc.)
- Can you buy space tickets in advance, or do you just set up and wait for someone to come around and collect the space rent? (Buying in advance will usually offer a better choice of spaces, hence the better location.)
- Are pets permitted? (Some swap meets permit them as long as they're on a leash or confined to the owner's space; others prohibit them.)
- Is change available at the office? (If you make a lot of sales, you could run out of change early in the day.)
- Is it possible to get onto the grounds prior to the official opening hour? (If you can get in early, you can be all set up before the first customers arrive.)
- Are selling spaces located on dirt, or are they paved? (If on dirt, be prepared to deal with dust or mud, depending on weather. Asphalt is hotter in warm weather.)
- Do they give rain checks? (Some smaller locations do. This simply means that if it rains, they will refund your space rent or allow you to set up free on another day.

Most large swap meets can't afford to give rain checks due to their high overhead.)

Last but not least, ask what time the rest rooms close. It's no fun tearing down three hours after they've closed, especially on a cold, wet, windy day!)

When the big day finally comes, try to arrive as early as possible. It will be easier to get into your space, especially if you drive a large pick-up or van. No one appreciates a late arrival asking, "Hey, buddy, can you move your tables so I can get my car in?" Arriving early also allows you to be set up and selling early, as previously mentioned. In this case, the early bird gets the dollars instead of the worm.

Dress comfortably but appropriately. In cold weather, dressing in layers will allow you to remove outer clothing as the temperature climbs. In warm weather, a layer of clothing is actually just as comfortable as the skimpiest of outfits. It's also better protection against sunburn. Consider personal appearance as well as comfort. No man looks good with three days' growth of beard and about six inches of beer gut hanging below a ragged, stained T-shirt. Very few women are actually attractive in short shorts and skimpy halters. In fact, a good many look downright disgusting in such outfits. Remember, the customer is supposed to reach for his wallet, not a barf bag.

Even if the swap meet has a snack bar, take something to eat and drink. You may be too busy to wait in line for a hamburger or Pepsi, or the snack bar could be too far away. Besides, food from home is cheaper and probably better. Most swap meet food is only adequate at best. A few have actual restaurants or cafeterias with very good food, but they are rare.

Take plenty of change, especially quarters and ones. This is particularly advisable if your selling space is near the entrance. A lot of customers allow themselves a $20 bill for shopping at the swap meet, or they come right after payday when a twenty may be the *smallest* bill they have. If you happen to be the first vendor they buy from, guess who has to change all those big bills! Other vendors are usually cooperative about making change in an emergency, but constant requests get old fast. A few times my wife and I have turned other vendors down simply because they made a habit of relying on others. "They set up here every weekend, so why do they have to ask us to break a twenty for their first sale *every* time?" we ask.

In addition to adequate change, try to have plenty of plastic bags on hand. It isn't necessary to go out and buy these, just recycle the ones from the supermarket. Customers appreciate a bag for their purchases, and it makes you look more professional. If you sell a lot of china and glassware, have newspapers handy for wrapping. Again, customers will appreciate the convenience and your thoughtfulness.

A few other supplies and some basic tools will often come in handy. A small tack hammer and an assortment of carpet tacks and nails can be used for minor repairs. Needle nose plies, a screwdriver, scissors, a measuring tape and utility knife are almost essential. Thumb tacks and push pins and a broad felt tip pen are always handy items to have in the tool box. We also carry a small battery tester, masking tape, a bottle of Elmer's wood glue, and a tube of Bond 527 jewelry and craft glue with us. An assortment of pens, pencils, erasers and a small notebook are practically essential. You can record sales, customer requests, information on other swap meets and sources of supply, etc., in a handy spiral notebook that fits easily into a shirt pocket. Depending on your individual situation, you may want to add other items to this basic list. Only time and experience will tell you what you do or don't need.

As mentioned earlier, we live in the Sun Belt, but our area is hardly immune from inclement weather. Even as I write these words, the aftermath of a hurricane in the Gulf of California is pushing a *lot* of moisture into the area. Heavy rains are expected statewide by morning. The National Weather Service is constantly updating the local and regional forecasts and broadcasting new flash flood and storm warning bulletins. The worst of the storms *should* be over by the upcoming weekend, but we aren't counting on it. In short, we're prepared for bad weather.

When working outdoors, we always have several long sheets of clear, 6 mil plastic with us. The weather forecast may sound perfect, but we know it can change drastically within minutes. This is especially true in the mountains in the summer. If necessary, we can cover our displays very quickly with the plastic and clamp it down against the wind. If it's only sprinkling, customers may still be out — and buying. There have been times when our sales totaled nearly $200 in a very short time under such conditions. We were able to make those sales simply because customers could still see the merchandise. Try doing that with an opaque blue tarp!

If you plan to set up regularly at a particular swap meet, be aware of the direction of the prevailing winds. A gentle breeze can be refreshing on a hot summer day, but facing into the wind on a cold, dreary winter day is definitely *not* an experience to be remembered with fondness.

Anyone who is particularly sensitive to sunshine should carry a good grade of suntan lotion and apply it liberally. A beach umbrella is good protection from the sun, but it should be tied or weighted down. A sudden gust of wind can blow it over, send it flying through the air to land a half mile away, or put it through a windshield of a car on the next aisle.

Don't be a space hog! If you need three selling spaces, pay for three. Don't expect to buy two, then fudge an extra couple of feet from the neighbor on each side. One-time yard salers are the worst offenders at this. I have, however, seen my share of so-called pros who made a habit of it. Last winter, a regular vendor at our winter location consistently bought only three spaces, then proceeded to try to maneuver his large motor home into them. In one case, the vendor next to him had to change her entire layout to accommodate a good five feet of motor home which projected into one of her spaces. Needless to say, she wasn't overly friendly toward her offending neighbor.

In addition to vendors who consistently buy less space than they actually need, I've also seen some who would set their tables right on the dividing line, then expect their neighbor to furnish them an aisle out of *his* space. Of course, if you see that the next vendor isn't using all of his space, it's perfectly alright to ask permission to use some of it. In return for the favor, offer to pay a share of his space rent. He will probably decline the offer, but at least you will have made the gesture. Believe me, it will be appreciated.

If you simply must take young children along while selling at the swap meet, keep them under observation, and control, at all times. Don't expect your neighbors to act as free baby-sitters. If the kids have to go to the rest room, take them. I once caught another vendor's youngster making a yellow puddle at the back of one of our spaces, right next to our merchandise boxes. A couple of hours later, he did it again. His parents were promptly informed that it had better not happen again. They could just get their knuckles up off the ground and take him to the rest room, otherwise we would file a formal complaint with the swap meet manager. They paid a little more attention to Junior after that, but not much. People like that can ruin your day!

As a potential vendor, you should be aware that some customers expect all prices to be negotiable. Some vendors will negotiate, others won't. If you *are* willing to negotiate, set the starting price higher than what you actually expect to get. You can then come down to the price you wanted in the first place, yet still give the customer the feeling they're getting a deal. Our policy is to remain firm on our prices, except in rare instances. After all, every time we give a customer a deal, we're actually taking money out of our pockets. If they complain about the price of an item, we simply say, "Lots of luck finding it elsewhere." Another effective line is, "This is a business, not a yard sale."

Sometimes the customer will go ahead and pay the asking price. In other cases, they will walk away, only to return a half hour to an hour later because they couldn't find the item elsewhere. Of course, we secretly gloat if it's been sold in the meantime. To carry the thought one step further, I have a friend who will actually hide an item if he sees a particularly obnoxious customer who has walked away returning for it. "Gee, I must have sold it," he tells them with a shrug. As they walk away empty-handed, he reaches under the table and retrieves the item they wanted. Of course, he loses a sale that way, but he also enjoys a moment of sweet revenge against a cheapskate who expected something for nothing.

While the advice contained in this chapter is by no means a complete guide to working swap meets, it does cover the basics of the business. More detailed information is contained in my earlier book, *How To Make Cash Money Selling At Swap Meets, Flea Markets, Etc.* (Loompanics Unlimited, 1988).

Most vendors who have been in the business for years agree that sales aren't nearly as lucrative as they used to be, especially from the late 1960s through the mid-1970s. Gone are the days when a vendor could start small and literally become wealthy within a few short years. It is, however, still possible to make good money with the right merchandise in the right location. Each year, the Independent Dealers Association, Inc., polls customers and vendors at various swap meets throughout the U.S. and Canada. Based on these ballots, they then compile a list of the Top 10 and Top 50 swap meets in North America and put it in their *Official Flea Market Directory.* As of this writing, the Top 10 markets are:

Apache Park 'N Swap, Apache Junction, Arizona
Rose Bowl Flea Market, Pasadena, California
The Flea Market, San Jose, California
Thunderbird Swap-Shop, Fort Lauderdale, Florida
Flea World, Orlando, Florida
Shipshewana Action & Flea Market, Shipshewana,
. Indiana
The Flea Market, Nashville, Tennessee
First Monday Trade Days, Canton, Texas
Traders Village, Grand Prairie, Texas (Dallas/Fort
Worth)
Rummage-O-Rama, Milwaukee, Wisconsin

For more information on the current *Official Flea Market Directory*, contact Independent Dealers Association by calling (314) 296-0989 or write them at PO Box 455, Arnold, MO 63010.

And Now, Plan B

Although swap meets are generally the best market-place for most people to sell used goods, they certainly aren't the only one. Certain types of merchandise are actually more suitable to other sales outlets. This is often true of special interest items which appeal only to a select clientele, but not always.

Some swap meets in the East have a reputation for being *the* place to shop for antiques. If you have a decent selection and live close by, consider trying one of these markets instead of just a run-of-the-mill swap meet, even if the latter draws a larger crowd. Remember, specialized selling is a numbers game. A large swap meet might attract 20,000 people on a given weekend, with only a few, if any, looking for antiques. The smaller one which is noted for antiques may only draw a crowd of 3,000, but a high percentage may be serious collectors. If you happen to have a particularly rare or desirable item, there may be anywhere from 10 to 100 potential buyers for it.

Targeting a particular clientele not only increases your sales potential, it also enables you to sell at a higher price. An original hood ornament for a 1937 Packard might attract little, if any, attention at a regular swap meet. If the asking price is $5, someone just *might* offer $2 for it, even if it's in perfect condition. Try selling it at an antique car show and see what happens! It probably wouldn't last a half hour at that price, or even at 10 times that much.

Again, the key is to have sufficient inventory to make working a specialty market worthwhile. You won't make a lot of money selling just one antique hood ornament, but what if you could sell 15 or 20? Of course, it's possible to have a successful show with only one sale, provided it's the *right* item. I observed this at a gun show several years ago. One dealer had a very large display of outstanding quality, yet he sold only one gun. It was an engraved, silver-plated single-action Colt revolver. Since it had been manufactured in the late 1880s or 1890s, it was a prized collector piece for that reason alone. What *really* pushed the selling price right through the roof was the accompanying letter of authenticity from the Colt factory. Their records showed that particular gun had been shipped to none other than Buffalo Bill Cody.

Gun shows are also an excellent place to sell antique swords, original or replica military uniforms from the 1800s, old spurs, chaps, saddles, etc. The key is for them to be actually collectable, not just old. Some gun shows permit the sale of such items, as well as coins, medals, Indian artifacts and anything else that can be lumped into a category known as Western Americana. Other shows limit merchandise to guns and gun-related items only, so do your homework before heading for the nearest gun show.

If you have a particularly desirable collection of old comic books, don't just haul them to the local swap meet. Look for a comicon (comic book convention) in your area, or contact a regular rare comics dealer and see what he will pay for the collection. Naturally, he will offer less than market value, as he has to make a profit when he re-sells them. But he will still offer far more than you could get at the swap meet. The same principle applies to science fiction magazines and paperbacks. If you have two or three banana boxes of old *Analogs,* don't just haul them to the swap meet. Take them to a science fiction convention. How long do you think a collection of *Star Trek* paperbacks would last at such a convention? Not very long, but they don't last long at a swap meet, either. It seems those Trekkies are *everywhere.*

If there are no specialty shows within a reasonable driving distance of home, don't despair. It's still possible to find buyers for unusual items without too much effort.

There seems to be at least one magazine, newspaper or newsletter devoted to virtually any special interest or hobby, no matter what it might be. Most of these publications run classified ads which are widely read by subscribers. Depending on the circulation, classified rates are often quite reasonable. It may be possible to find just the right magazine at the local supermarket, or you may have to do some serious looking. When you find the publication you want, turn to the classified section and look under the appropriate heading. A typical ad in *Model Railroader* might read:

```
            LIONEL WANTED
I pay top dollar for pre-1950 Lionel trains
and accessories in good to mint condition.
    Send list, prices and SASE for reply.
   Ray's Switch Yard, 1234 Pacific Blvd.,
          Watsonville, CA 98765.
```

Like the comic book dealer, Ray won't offer as much as a private collector. If he's reputable, and he probably is, he will still offer a fair wholesale price.

If you don't have a collectable Lionel set, but have American Flyer instead, write to Ray anyway. Tell him what you have and how much you want for it, or ask if he's interested and what he would pay. Include an SASE (self-addressed, stamped envelope) with your letter. You might never receive a reply, or you might hear from Ray within a few days. Be sure to include your phone number. If Ray if *really* interested, he might want to call and discuss your equipment in detail before making an offer.

Of course, you can always run an ad in a special interest publication yourself, no matter what you want to sell. It doesn't take an Ernest Hemingway to write an effective ad. Just include all essential information, but keep the ad short and to the point. A typical ad which might attract the attention of private collectors and dealers alike might read:

```
        LIONEL 1947 FREIGHT SET
    Steam loco, light & smoke, eight cars.
  Near new in original box. Book value $2500.
            Sacrifice at $1800 OBO.
    Stan Biloxi, 4567 Willow Grove Rd.,
            Poughkeepsie, NY 12345.
```

Of course, there are ads, and there are ads. Imagine being able to run the following ad in virtually *any* collector-oriented magazine:

```
      JOHN WAYNE AUTOGRAPHED STILLS
    8 x 10 glossies from all his movies,
          autographed by the Duke.
      Some have other autographs as well.
    Entire set $1500 (will not split) firm.
      Stan Biloxi, 4567 Willow Grove Rd.,
            Poughkeepsie, NY 12345.
```

Would someone actually pay that much for a bunch of old movie photos? You'd better believe it! Last year, a friend of mine visited one of the major studios in Hollywood and paid $500 for a mixed lot of movie stills.

Within 24 hours after his return home, he sold the entire batch to a movie collectibles and nostalgia dealer for $5,000. And there wasn't a single autograph or John Wayne picture in the entire lot!

Used Clothing

Good used clothing is always in demand, no matter what the present economic climate. If you doubt this, simply visit the nearest thrift shop, especially on sale day. The clothing department is *always* the busiest in the store.

The popular misconception of thrift shop customers is of a wino shopping for something that isn't *quite* as shabby as what he's already wearing. Nothing could be further from the truth. Winos spend any money they have on *wine*, with food running a poor second. Clothing and shelter are even further down their priority list.

Based on personal observation, I can safely state that the average used clothing customer is either a young, low-income mother with small children, or a retiree trying to survive on just a Social Security check. As one mother was overheard to say, "Kids outgrow things so fast I can't afford to buy them new clothes. Here, I can get them something decent to wear for fifty cents or a dollar." She was actually quite fortunate to find clothes for her brood at those prices, even on sale day. Most used clothing in thrift shops is priced considerably higher, yet it's still cheaper than buying new, even at discount stores. And most is in good condition, with some items almost brand new in appearance.

Most affluent people discard clothing in good condition for a number of reasons. Gaining or losing a significant amount of weight is probably the most common reason. Kids outgrow their clothes rather quickly, and there may not be a younger brother or sister to wear their hand-me-downs. Sometimes people discard perfectly good clothes because they're drastically out of style, or they may just be tired of them. They might change jobs or lifestyles, or move to a different climate. Obviously, someone moving from Minnesota or Alaska to Hawaii won't take thermal underwear and a heavy parka with them.

Sometimes a person who earns a good salary will buy clothing at a thrift shop for special purposes. Painters, printers, auto mechanics and other working people whose occupations can result in stained clothing are often hesitant to pay high prices for new work clothes.

In the late 1970s, I had a job which required me to function in a variety of capacities, both white-collar and blue-collar. I might literally have breakfast with a U.S. Senator and a Representative in the morning, pick up a wealthy client at the airport just before lunch, run a printing press in the afternoon, then go the local TV station to film a commercial that night. Obviously, I didn't want to drive the boss's brand new Lincoln to the airport with printer's ink on my clothes, nor did I want to risk getting ink or darkroom chemicals on a white shirt or dress slacks. I would usually report for work dressed for a day in the office area, but always had a set of older clothing hanging in the men's room of the print shop "just in case." The latter were actually presentable clothes from the sale table of the local discount store, but they could just as easily have come from a thrift shop. I could wear them in the office if I had to, but it didn't matter if I got ink on them.

When I changed jobs a few years later, the white shirts and sports coats were relegated to the back area of the closet, worn only for weddings and funerals. Although my new employer was a very successful and profitable publishing company, the dress code was strictly casual. In fact, the owner usually wore bib overalls and high-topped work shoes. Cammies and Levi's were considered perfectly acceptable attire for both men and women at all times. Needless to say, I went shopping for a set of cammies at the nearest surplus store.

Obviously, the most lucrative market for used clothing is infants' and children's wear. If you doubt it, just look at the birth announcements in the local newspaper. There are literally millions of babies born in this country every year, and every one of them comes into the world stark naked. Within a year's time, each may go through three or four sizes of infant wear. As they continue to grow, they *grow*. Some mothers purposely buy children's clothing one size too large to get more wear from them, but the kids still outgrow them eventually.

Many swap meet vendors who sell used clothing buy their inventory at thrift shops, but not all of them do. I have a friend who sells nothing but military surplus clothing, web gear, and camping equipment. While he buys some of his merchandise from a large surplus wholesaler, a lot of his clothing comes directly from military personnel who are being mustered out.

Another fellow I know buys "retired" uniforms from the city, removes the municipal insignia, and sells them at the local swap meet. They are useless for trying to impersonate a police officer or other city employee, but are perfectly adequate for painting a house, mowing the lawn or rebuilding an automobile engine or transmission.

A variation of selling used clothing is to sell new, discontinued items. The very first professional vendor I ever knew did exactly that. He bought nothing but discontinued salesmen's samples. It didn't matter if they were shoes, men's dress slacks, or ladies' undies. If they were new and discontinued, he would buy them. When one sales rep asked him if he could actually make a living doing that, the vendor told him what his average profit was for two days of selling. "Golly," the salesman replied. "You work fewer hours, and make more than I do!"

Small Appliances & Household Goods

To many people, Benjamin Franklin was just a funny-looking guy whose picture now appears on the hundred dollar bill. But to those interested in electronics, he is probably best remembered for having an electrifying experience.

It seems his friend, Tom Edison, was slowly going blind from working long hours in his laboratory with no light save a dim kerosene lantern. Ben thought new glasses might help Tom, so he broke a couple of beer bottles, wrapped a little wire around the pieces, and invented bifocals. When these failed to help, Tom gave him a little friendly advice: "Ben, you're a nice guy. You're fun at parties and your picture would look great on a hundred dollar bill. But as an optician you just don't make it. Why don't you go fly a kite?"

Not wanting to hurt Tom's feelings, Ben decided to follow his advice. Since it was a stormy day, he was afraid he might get locked out in the rain, so he tied his house key to the end of the kite string. *Zappo!* Lightning struck the kite, traveled down the string, hit the key, bounced across the picket fence through the window of Tom Edison's laboratory. There it hit a glass globe that Tom used to store odds and ends of wire, and the electric light was born.

It didn't really happen that way, of course, but that's the way Hollywood might present the story. In reality, Ben Franklin *purposely* flew his kite on a stormy day in

1752 to prove lightning was, indeed, electricity. Edison's invention of the electric light bulb was hardly an accident, but rather the result of months of research and painstaking labor in 1879. Among Edison's other accomplishments, he also designed the first electric power station, thus paving the way for electricity to become available to millions of people.

Thanks to Ben Franklin, Tom Edison, and a host of nameless inventors and engineers, we now live in an electronic age which was undreamed of just a few short years ago. In the 1960s, electric typewriters were a marvel. Today, many grade school students wouldn't even recognize one. To them, it would be just some kind of dinosaur that predated PCs, or personal computers. In fact, last year's computer models are practically dinosaurs to many people. Their technology may actually be far beyond what most people need, but they are virtually unsaleable because they aren't the *latest* model. If you doubt this, consider the case of a dealer I recently met at a ham radio gathering. He sold computer components, and had several late-model terminals he was trying to sell at very low prices. They were brand new, still in the factory cartons, and he had gotten them free. A friend of his who owned a computer store had written them off, then given them to him. "If you don't take them," his friend said, "I'll just throw them in the Dumpster."

While not everyone has a PC, or even wants or needs one, they are becoming extremely common. Just how common was borne out by a newscast I watched the other night. A lady who lives in a very remote rural area was ecstatic that the local power company was finally going to run lines to her house. "Now I don't have to worry about my computer going down because the generator ran out of gas," she said.

Computers aside, most Americans use a wide variety of electronic gadgets every day. Rather than slave over a hot stove, they pop a frozen dinner in the microwave so they can have more time to watch TV. They throw their dirty clothes in an electric washing machine, then an hour or so later pop them in the electric dryer. Before they go to bed at night, they brush with an electric toothbrush, set an electric alarm clock, then turn out the lights.

Even low-income families take many electronic labor-saving and entertainment devices for granted. If they can't afford new ones, they visit auctions, thrift stores and swap meets in search of good, used TV's, VCR's, vacuum cleaners, etc.

There are a number of swap meet vendors who specialize in electronics and electrical appliances. Some sell nothing but TV's and VCR's while others sell stereos, kitchen gadgets or small kitchen appliances. I know one fellow who sells used vacuum cleaners. As a sideline, he also sells vacuum cleaner bags and replacement hoses. Another repairs electric razors, but he also sells reconditioned ones. Yet another fellow who sells kitchen appliances has a lucrative sideline in such non-electrical items as mixing bowls, storage containers, dishes, etc.

The list of small appliances and household items for which there is a used market is endless, but some of the more popular items include:

- Electric toasters & toaster ovens
- Mr. Coffee machines & percolators
- Crock pots, microwaves & electric skillets

- Vacuum cleaners
- Hot air popcorn poppers
- Electric can openers
- TV's, radios, stereos, VCR's, etc. (Video movies are a good sideline to the latter while audio tapes & LP records don't sell nearly as well.)
- Small power tools (drills, chain saws, sanders, etc.)

As with any type of merchandise, gear your electronics to the local area. Hot air popcorn poppers won't sell all that well in areas where most of the clientele wears dentures. They *will* sell where there is an abundance of teenagers or families with small children.

Naturally, whatever you sell should be in good working order. If you sell at a swap meet, and electricity is available, be prepared to demonstrate appliances to potential customers. Nothing will sell a used vacuum cleaner faster than watching it pull dust and debris from a small section of carpet (often available free from carpet stores). If it's a hot day, give yourself a cool breeze with an electric fan. In cold weather, brew yourself a pot of hot coffee. The smell alone will probably attract customers. One might very well come along and say, "I don't want the Mr. Coffee that's on the table, I want the one you're using. That one obviously works."

Paperback Books

As mentioned previously, my wife and I sell used paperbacks at the local swap meet in the winter. We also sell them at a few select locations during the summer, but not at every location we work, nor every weekend. Remember, *to maximize sales, know your clientele.*

Of course, a lot of swap meet vendors *think* they're in the book business. "You sell books, too?" one commented last winter. "I sell a lot of books. I sold three thousand out here last summer."

On the surface, that statement would seem to say a lot. It does, but it's actually more negative than positive. At that particular swap meet, 3,000 books is a large number to sell in the summer. There are very few vendors due to the heat, but also very few customers. However, further questioning revealed just how that vendor was able to sell so many books. He would pay $1 to $2 for a mixed lot of paperbacks at the local auction, then put them out at 25 cents each. Although his profit margin was good, his actual gross sales were very low, even by summer standards. Assuming he was able to work both Friday and Saturday nights for all 25 weekends, that would give him average gross sales of $15 per night for all 50 nights. Frankly, the poor guy would have had apoplexy if he had known what our average daily sales were during the winter months. One Saturday in February alone, our book sales nearly equaled his total for the entire summer! Days such as that are very, very rare, but our winter sales are still consistently quite good.

Until the preceding year, we had been selling nothing but new goods. We were quite happy with that arrangement for several years. When the state of the economy forced our sales downward, we had to find a solution to the problem — *muy Pronto*. We needed a sure-fire winner for the upcoming winter, preferably something that would require only a small capital investment. A personal interest in and knowledge of the merchandise would also be beneficial, if not downright essential. Since my wife has a Master's degree in library science and I spent over 20 years in various aspects of the publishing business, used paperbacks were a logical choice. However, in making this choice we were breaking three of our own rules for success:

1. Never mix used goods with new. (It will cheapen the appearance of the overall display, plus give customers the idea they can haggle on all prices.)
2. Never add a new line which is totally unrelated to your present merchandise. (It 's far better to merely increase the variety or add a complementary line. For example, add jewelry or cosmetics to ladies' clothing, not fishing tackle, rock star posters or automotive supplies.)
3. Never add a type of merchandise for which the market is already saturated. (In other words, avoid competition. In our case, there were already several paperback dealers at the swap meet.)

There is, of course, a fourth rule, most often applied to the arts. It's perfectly okay to break a rule to achieve a specific goal, provided you realize you are breaking it.

Fortunately, we knew what we were doing, or at least thought we did. We made a few mistakes, the biggest being in *under*estimating our sales potential. Any business would welcome that type of mistake!

My wife's biggest mistake was assuming science fiction in general would be a top seller. She likes to read it, and knew the local used book stores charged a premium for used SF. She misjudged the market for our clientele, and we went into the season with a lot of titles that didn't sell.

My mistake was in warning her away from the more raunchy series Westerns. "The Gunslammer No. 413: *Wayward Wenches Of Wichita?*" I would shout when looking at her latest purchases. "That's garbage! Get some *good* Westerns." The good Westerns sold extremely well that winter. In fact, we were completely sold out of any kind of Western for several weeks early in the season. But we also had numerous requests for some of the raunchy series. For awhile, it seemed the likes of *Wayward Wenches Of Wichita* and *Amorous Annie Of Abilene* were the most requested Western titles of all time.

Despite a few early mistakes, we persevered — and prospered. Within a few days, we had recouped our entire initial investment and were operating in the profit column. It was also apparent we didn't have to worry much about competition. We *were* the competition. To understand how we were able to achieve this success in such a short time, a little background information is in order.

We decided to diversify into used paperbacks for the winter early the preceding May. At the time, we were selling at a different swap meet in another part of the state. It was basically a used goods market, so there was no shortage of yard salers with paperback books. Their prices were usually quite cheap, so we knew we could re-sell the books at a good profit. Although our cash flow was tight at the time, we invested a few dollars each weekend to build our future inventory. Normally, my wife would visit the yard salers as soon as they set up, then bring her purchases back to our stand. If business was slow, I would start cleaning and pricing the books while she went looking for more. Sometimes she was able to buy an entire banana box full for $5, and just three of the books inside would be worth that much. If necessary, we could throw half the box away and still make a nice profit on the remainder.

After doing this for several weeks, we had accumulated quite a few books that were too good to throw away, yet they didn't fit the standards we wanted to sell. Remember, we were looking strictly for quality at the time, or at least instant saleability, not just quantity. We solved the surplus problem by taking the books we didn't want to a used book store that traded one of theirs for two of ours. At the time, we rarely paid more than a dime per book, and we could sell their books and make a profit.

By the end of the summer season, we had an inventory of between 1,500 and 2,000 books in our garage. Our total cash outlay was less than $500. Categories included romance, mystery, non-fiction war, Westerns, historical and frontier novels, science fiction, and a handful of biographies and true crime titles. The books had already been cleaned and priced, so it was now only necessary to box and label them according to category.

The local Avon dealer offered us an unlimited supply of empty boxes, so we decided to use them rather than the usual banana boxes. Avon boxes were smaller and held fewer books, but they were much lighter and easier to lift and carry. I cut each box to a height of three and a half inches. That was enough to protect the books, yet allow a customer to easily remove the titles he or she wanted. I then made cardboard signs for each category and placed each in the top of a box within the appropriate category. When we opened the boxes at the swap meet, it was a simple matter to stand each sign upright at the rear of a row of boxes. This enabled customers to find the category they wanted without wading through numerous boxes of irrelevant material. "I love the way your boxes are organized," customers would say. "I can actually find what I want without asking."

Initially, we priced our books at roughly one-third the original cover price. That didn't last long. What we *thought* might be an entire winter's supply of books was badly depleted after only three or four weekends. When we had to restock locally, we had to pay a lot more for our purchases. We could *still* make a small profit at our old selling price, but that would have been counterproductive. After all, it took a lot of time and gas to find the books, plus more time and effort to clean and price them.

Our original price scale was also cheap enough that a couple of other dealers would buy certain titles from us, then resell them at a profit. "I'm not about to run around and get their inventory for them," my wife said. "I'm going to raise the prices on those books to match theirs." I then added my two cents' worth. "We're not about to do all that work for the small profit we're making now," I said. I immediately devised a new price scale, with most books selling for 25 cents less than half the cover price. In other words, a $6 book now sold for $2.75, tax included, rather than the $2 we had originally charged.

Despite what may seem like a drastic price increase, we were still cheaper than the used book stores — and a couple of other dealers at the swap meet. Titles which were less than six months old went up to half the cover price, as did those by certain popular authors which we could hardly keep in stock. We received very few complaints about the increase in price. Customers who did complain were looking for cheap rather than quality, anyway, and probably would have complained about our old prices. They expected our books to be 50 cents each, or 5 for $1, like the junk a so-called competitor had been trying to unload for over two years.

As the season progressed, our book sales continued to increase beyond all expectations. It soon became a major undertaking just trying to keep up with the demand. Our weekday schedule soon developed into a somewhat hectic but workable routine. On Mondays, my wife would leave home early in order to canvass the thrift shops which stocked their book shelves on that day. She would usually arrive home shortly after dark with a large load. On Tuesday, she would visit another group of thrift shops while I cleaned and priced Monday's purchases. Wednesday found me processing Tuesday's load while she again made a book run. On Thursday, we would both clean and price Wednesday's batch, then file all the books in the appropriate category.

At this point, it's appropriate to mention a little trick we call "creative misfiling." This is, quite simply, purposely misfiling a book in what would seem to be the wrong category. As an example, we put Agatha Christie's autobiography in the mystery section rather than among the other biographies. Louis L'Amour's memoirs, when we can get a copy, automatically go in Westerns. If his book of poetry, *Smoke At The Altar*, ever becomes available in standard paperback format, it will go in Westerns, too. Our reasoning is quite simple: Agatha Christie fans will look in the mystery boxes for their reading material, not in the biography section. Since few of them know she even wrote her autobiography, they will get a very pleasant surprise and we'll have an instant sale. A person who normally reads poetry might not buy a book of poems by Louis L'Amour, but any hard-core L'Amour fan will buy it *immediately!* It's the one book that's usually missing from their collection.

After selling books for several weekends, it became readily apparent that some categories and authors were far more popular than we had anticipated. Others were a disappointment. It took time to change our setup, but we accommodated our customers' wishes as quickly as we could. We cut back on some of the romances and increased the historical novel section, which has proven to be our single most popular category. We also increased the true crime section from one box to four, then eventually cut it back to three then we discovered some titles were consistent sellers, others weren't.

We were surprised one day when a customer picked out a true crime book and told us he would take every copy of that title we could get. He was the detective who caught the mass murderer in the book, and he even showed us his picture on page 183. He was younger then, but the picture was definitely him!

In another case, an elderly gentleman asked us to find a particular book about the Vietnam War. Again, he said he would take every copy we could get. One chapter was devoted to the firefight in which his son won the Medal of Honor, and a portion of the chapter dealt exclusively with him. The book was out of print, and not all of the relatives had a copy yet. It took several months, but we were able to get a copy for the father. We're still looking for others.

Keeping up with customers' demands for new titles kept us busy trying to guess what they might want next. When *Scarlett* was finally released in paperback, we began stockpiling every copy of *Gone With The Wind* we could find in decent condition. It paid off, as we sold out quickly.

Unlike most swap meet paperback dealers, we set up a trade policy whereby customers could trade books they had already read for ones they hadn't. We take two of theirs, plus 25 cents, for each of our books they take out. Of course, we don't just take any book in trade, only those authors and titles we can use. This isn't much of a problem, as we quite often get books back that we sold just the preceding weekend. In many cases, they're titles we desperately need and we're only too glad to get them. Occasionally, a customer will look at a stack of traders we've rejected and say, "Aw, go ahead and keep them. I don't want to carry them around." If that happens, we usually waive the 25 cent surcharge. After all, we can usually trade those books somewhere else.

We also do special book searches for customers. Our fee for this service is 25 cents above our regular selling price. After all, if we're looking for books anyway, it doesn't take that long to try to find a particular title. No one has *ever* complained about the fee. They usually laugh because it's so low.

Several times, customers have asked us to assemble a complete set of the *Wagons West* series for them, or to find certain titles they're missing from another series. "I want to read them, but not until I have them all," they say. When this happens, we automatically waive the 25 cent search fee. After all, the total sale might amount to $50, so we believe the customer is entitled to a little special consideration. We also waive the fee when we get requests for multiple copies of a single title, as in the cases of the detective and the soldier's father mentioned above.

When selling books, it helps to know as many different authors and titles as you can, even if you don't normally carry them. Not too long ago, a customer asked where he should look for books by Glendon Swarthout. "We don't have anything by him right now," I answered, "but we had *The Shootist* and *They Came To Cordura* a couple of weeks ago." The customer was obviously impressed. "Well, at least *you* know who I'm talking about," he replied. Obviously, he had asked several other book dealers for that author and had received nothing but blank stares for a reply. Does that mean my wife and I know every title there is to know? Certainly not! With approximately 130 books being published *every day* in the United States alone, that's an impossible task. But we do try to stay abreast of the current best sellers as well as some of the more popular older authors and titles.

In addition to knowing authors and titles, it helps to know how authors' names are pronounced. Louis L'Amour is "Louie", not "Lewis." Michael Crichton's last name is pronounced "Cryton," while Ken Follett is actually "Foe-lay." Of course, some authors like Danielle Steele are also pronounced "megabucks" for themselves, their publishers, their agents, and the book sellers. If you don't know who *she* is, stay out of the book business!

In addition to all the aforementioned, we have several other advantages over the other book dealers at the swap meet.

We're on the bottom row, next to the parking lot, and are located right next to one of only two entrances at that end of the swap meet. Ours is the first book setup customers see when they come in, and the last before they leave.

The other book dealers operate in the open, or at the very most have a canopy to shade themselves. Our setup is under a large, spacious canopy (almost 800 square feet). This not only protects the books from the sun, it isolates our setup from those around it. It fairly invites customers to come in and browse in a leisurely manner. The longer they browse, the more they buy. It's not at all unusual to have a customer browse for a half hour, bring a large stack of books over to our checkout table, then go back for more. People like that can definitely make your day!

We readily accept personal checks, travelers' checks and major credit cards. Customers tend to buy more if they know they can charge it or write a check, saving their cash for emergencies or other purchases.

Not only are our books clean, they also aren't likely to fall apart. If a book is losing its cover or there are loose pages, I glue them back together. This works on most books, but not on some of the more recent ones.

Sometime in the early 1990s, publishers began looking for a way to sabotage the used book business. New book sales were down, they claimed, because too many people were buying used paperbacks. (Of course, people buy used books because new ones are too expensive, or publishers no longer stock the titles they want. Only the best selling authors have their books perpetually in print.) Some sneaky rascal came up with the idea of using a special "break-away" glue. This was meant to hold a book together only long enough to be read once. It was also designed so no other glue would adhere to the dried "break-away" glue. The system backfired, as many books fell apart before the original purchaser could finish reading them. Needless to say, they complained to the stores which sold them the books. Most store owners refunded the customers their money, then sent the books back to the publisher. Hopefully, "break-away" glue is now a thing of the past, or at least will be until they can devise a way to make it work.

There is one particular glue that will defeat "break-away" glue, but I won't mention its name for two reasons. First, the EPA, FDA or some other bureaucracy might ban it if they find out it works. Second, publishers would know exactly which glue they needed to render ineffective, thus making their research easier.

Running a successful used paperback business is a lot of hard, constant work, but it can be profitable. It can also be personally satisfying, especially when it evokes customer comments like the following:

"Your books are so clean. Are they new?"

"I don't even bother to check the other book dealers anymore. You usually have what I want, and your books are always in such good condition."

"This is wonderful (as they look at our signs)! I can actually find what I want here."

"I'm buying all my L'Amour books from you from now on. You're cheaper than the other guys, and your books are in a lot better shape." (The swap meet is strictly a seller's market when it comes to Louis L'Amour. Some dealers charge $2 each, regardless of original cover price or condition. We charge $1 for them in poor condition, a minimum of $1.50 in good condition. Later editions with higher cover prices are half the original price. Of course, rare, early editions would be much higher. A first edition of *Hondo*, with the famous endorsement from John Wayne, would carry a $75 to $100 asking price, firm. If autographed by the author, we would ask even more for it, provided my wife could find where I hid it on my own bookshelf!)

Of course, my favorite customer is a guy who comes by every Saturday morning and complains, "Got anything I haven't read yet?" My stock reply, half jokingly and half-seriously, is, "Gil, not even the Library of Congress has something you haven't read yet." An exaggeration, to be sure, but it is extremely difficult to find a historical novel he hasn't read. It's also a lot of fun on those rare occasions when we're able to surprise him with a new title.

Honest John's Used Cars

Recently, a friend commented that her family was quite concerned about the fate of her uncle. He was an unemployed aerospace engineer. With the Cold War virtually ended and the attendant reduction in military spending, his prospects for employment in that field in the near future were virtually nil.

During the course of the conversation, she also commented that he had just bought an old pickup, made some minor repairs and resold it at a $1,500 profit. From the day he bought the pickup until he resold it was less than a week.

"Is he a good mechanic?" my wife asked.

"He's great!" our friend replied. "He can fix just about anything."

"So what's he worried about?" my wife continued. "He should be able to make a living."

She was thinking, of course, that he should be able to recycle just about any kind of electrical or mechanical item, from toasters to cars and pickups. The price of new cars has increased dramatically in the last few years, placing them beyond the financial reach of many people who could previously afford them. High unemployment and an overall poor economy haven't helped their sales, either. The demand for good used cars remains strong. People *do* still replace their old vehicle when necessary. Maybe the old car just finally wore out, or a growing family now requires moving up from a compact to a station wagon or van. More often than not, these people begin looking for a good used car before considering a new one. They may actually *want* a new car, but are practical enough to realize they simply can't afford it. After all, it's a lot easier to come up with $5,000 to $8,000 than $15,000 to $25,000.

At this point, the backyard car salesman may enter the picture. Not everyone buys a used car from regular dealers, all of whom claim, "We keep only the good ones and wholesale out the clunkers." In fact, a lot of people turn to the classified ads *first,* or buy publications such as *Auto Trader, Pickup Marketplace,* etc. For those unfamiliar with them, these are simply advertising outlets for used cars, trucks, motorcycles, boats, etc. In urban areas, the local convenience store probably carries several titles. Each will feature of number of ads from both regular dealers and private individuals. A few of the latter aren't really selling the old family jalopy. They regularly buy, fix up, and sell used cars at a profit.

In my home state, the practice has become so common that the used car dealers pressured the legislature into action. They could hardly ban such sales, so they passed a law requiring anyone who purchased a car or truck from an individual to pay sales tax on the transaction when they reregistered the vehicle in their name.

Frankly, I doubt if the new law hurt backyard car sales that much, but it did create some interesting situations. A lady I worked with at the time bought an eight-year-old Cadillac from her brother for $100. "Nobody at the registration office is going to believe what you paid for that car," I told her.

The story might have ended there, but that was just the start of it. At the time her brother offered her the car, Sally didn't have $100 with which to buy it. "I'll give you $100 for your old car," another co-worker told her. Sally gladly accepted his offer. He cleaned her old car up, made a few minor repairs, and resold it within a few days for $350. The month before, he bought and resold a little Toyota station wagon at a profit. A couple of weeks before that, it was an American compact. While he wasn't getting rich as a backyard car salesman, he made enough money at it to make the payments on his wife's *new* car. Eventually, his experience at such transactions enabled him to obtain a full-time job with a large dealership in another state. The last I knew, he was earning about $70,000 per year selling cars, a *lot* more than he made at his old job.

Before attempting to run a backyard used car lot, check state and local laws regarding licensing, title registration, insurance, etc. Some states allow a certain time period before registering a car in your name. If you can buy, repair and resell a car within the time limit, you can save yourself a lot of paperwork. The limit is 10 days in my home state, but that may not be the magic number in yours.

Used car dealers like to advertise their cars as being "$500 below book" or "$2,000 below book." This means the price is that much below the national average market value as listed in the *Kelly Blue Book*. The book will list both high and low values, depending on condition, optional equipment, etc.

The *Blue Book* is used mainly by dealers, insurance adjusters and bank loan officers. It gives them a ball park value for a specific vehicle, but doesn't necessarily reflect regional values. In our area, pickups and vans generally hold their value much better than compacts or standard-sized sedans. Extended cab pickups are especially popular, as they often serve double duty. They may haul hay or a stock trailer on the ranch during the week, then take the entire family into town on the weekends. In large urban areas, compacts and other "town" cars are in greater demand.

Some auto magazines also publish an annual guide to used car prices. Again, these are ball park figures, not Holy Writ. They will, however, give some indication of what a specific, late-model used car is worth. Don't pay the top price shown, then expect to resell at a profit, especially if any repairs are needed.

When looking for used cars to buy for resale, always look for the deal which offers the highest final profit margin. This isn't just the difference between your buying and selling prices. It includes cost of repairs, the time it takes to do them, any advertising you might do, and the probability of an immediate resale. In short, multiples of quick sales at a smaller profit margin with the least amount of work may put more money in your pocket than hoping for a high-profit sale several months down the road. If you simply *must* restore that '55 Thunderbird or '57 Chevy Bel-Air, go ahead and do it. (More on restoration in a later chapter.) In the meantime don't ignore the profits of buying and reselling plain old "transportation," which is what most people actually need.

One often overlooked aspect of buying and reselling cars is the "parting out" of a wrecked car, or an older one. If one can be bought for a bargain price, but it would cost too much to fix it up, consider the possibility of buying it and then selling the individual pieces. Salvageable engines, transmissions, wheels, etc., from a fairly popular model are always worth money.

My barber works a variation of the backyard used car lot, specializing in RV's. In the spring, he buys travel trailers and small motor homes from snowbirds who are getting ready to leave for the summer. He cleans them up, makes minor repairs, then sells them to local residents who are planning the family vacation or weekend camping trips. When the locals are ready to sell after Labor Day, he buys them back, repeats the cleaning and repair process, and resells them to returning snowbirds. He seldom has to advertise his product. Most of his customers come right out of his barber chair.

One last word of advice. If you aren't mechanically inclined, don't even consider going into the used car business. The cost of professional repairs, even minor ones, can become *very* expensive.

Seasonal Merchandise

Although certainly not the most important aspect of selling used merchandise, seasonal items do deserve mention. By "seasonal," I don't just mean Christmas or Easter items, although they may well be worth carrying at the right time of year. There won't, however, be much demand for Styrofoam Santas, Christmas tree ornaments or plywood silhouette Easter bunnies in July.

Certain types of clothing are obviously seasonal, with swimsuits selling best when the weather turns warm in the spring. Depending on the section of the country, kids' jackets may sell well as early as Labor Day, or the season may start as late as Thanksgiving. As with warm clothing, blankets and electric heaters will sell best right after the first few cool evenings in the fall. Conversely, I *have* seen electric heaters sell in August when the temperature was 110°. In that particular case, the guy selling them was a yard saler cleaning out his garage, *not* a professional vendor. He let the two he had go for $1 each, so he obviously wasn't trying to make a profit. The person who bought them did so because the price was right, not because he anticipated using them that same evening.

Remember, most people who are shopping for used goods don't have a lot of extra money. They can't afford to buy a winter item in May just because it's cheap. They'll be looking for swimsuits, camping gear and ice chests, not toboggans and sleds. An exception might be ice skates, provided there is an indoor rink nearby. In my area, it's too warm even in January to go ice skating outdoors. That's still fishing and water skiing weather to some people!

Golf clubs will sell better in the New England states or Minnesota in the summer months than in winter, but they're a hot item in my area when the snow flies up north. Many snowbirds buy a set when they arrive and use them all winter. I know, because I've seen snowbirds in tank tops and shorts playing the local course in January. Like all the other locals, I'm wearing a flannel shirt and parka on a cold January day.

When the snowbirds go home in the spring, they either sell their clubs at a yard sale or sell them back to the dealer they bought them from. There are two *large* used golf club setups at the local swap meet, and both do well. One is run by a retired pro while the other is the domain of a fairly young lady who still gives golf lessons during the week. Needless to say, both know their merchandise and are fully qualified to help customers select the set of clubs that is most appropriate for their needs.

One need only go 150 miles away to find an area where golf clubs sell best at the beginning of summer. The same applies to outboard motors and fishing tackle. From about the beginning of August until the middle of September, golf clubs and fishing tackle steadily decline in popularity. Used rifles, shotguns and compound bows suddenly become the hottest items for men. Since the area is located in the mountains, it's easy to understand this shift in sales. Tourists and summer residents buy the golf clubs and fishing tackle. As they leave in the fall, local residents turn their attention to the upcoming hunting season. In this case, the men tend to buy a little early so they can practice with their new weapons. They also shop early for the best selection, as they know the swap meet will soon close due to cold weather. Camping out when it's 10° below zero so you can hunt the early morning feeding grounds may be macho and fun. But go shopping outdoors in the of weather? No way!

Nostalgia Breeds $$$$$

Everybody wants to go to Grandma's house, especially little Joey. While the appeal for the rest of the family is Grandma's oatmeal cookies, for Joey it's the lure of her attic. He's heard plenty of stories about how Grandma never threw anything away, especially when Uncle Oscar went off to war in 1942. She just *knew* Uncle Oscar would never come home, so she carefully stored all his things away in the attic. She couldn't bear to look at them, but she couldn't bear to part with them, either.

Of course, Uncle Oscar did come home, but then he went off to college to study under the GI Bill. He met a girl there, got married, and moved to Houston after graduation. For years, he kept writing Grandma that he would clean out the attic during his vacation "someday." That day never arrived, and now Uncle Oscar has completely forgotten all those memories so carefully preserved in the attic. But Joey has heard about them, and he can't wait until vacation time so he can visit Grandma's house.

Of course, Grandma is actually his great-grandmother, and Uncle Oscar is Joey's great uncle, but those facts are immaterial. What matters is there is probably a lot of really neat, old stuff buried in the dust and cobwebs of that famous attic. Joey has never heard the word "nostalgia," but he knows treasures when he sees them.

Finally, the great day arrives. Although everyone has spent weeks cautioning Joey to be polite and not press the subject of the attic, he can hardly contain his curiosity. After only two oatmeal cookies, he blurts out, "Grandma, can I go look at the stuff in your attic?" Everyone else is properly embarrassed, but not Grandma. After all, what are great-grandchildren for, if not to be indulged? She escorts Joey upstairs to the guest room, lowers the disappearing stairway in the ceiling, and turns on the attic light. Joey scrambles eagerly up the stairs.

At first, he's crestfallen. All he sees is a dusty, tattered old dressmaker's dummy, a stack of yellowed and ragged newspapers, and a broken console radio. Then, in a far corner, he spies a large steamer trunk and several very old cardboard boxes.

Carefully, almost reverently, he lifts the lid to see the trunk and peers inside. The first thing he sees is a record album, but not like the ones he's used to. It's a true album, with four or five different records in paper jackets. Each record has only one song to a side, and the records are thick and heavy. They also look like they have never been played, so the orchestra must not have been any good. Joey makes a mental note to ask Grandma who Glenn Miller was.

Joey has been so intent on looking at the records that he hasn't even noticed what lay below. As he sets the album aside, his eyes bulge at the sight of the comic books. *Wow!* The Mother Lode, the Holy Grail and Mecca all rolled into one! There, right on top, is the very first issue of *Superman!* Joey has no idea what it's worth, but he knows it must be plenty. ("Hey, Grandma, you wanna buy a new Cadillac?") Joey lifts the Man of Steel almost reverently from the top of the stack, then glances quickly through the rest of the comics. Nothing else looks familiar, except one featuring Mickey Mouse. *That* Mickey looks nothing like the one he knows today.

Beneath the comic books, Joey finds a Lionel train set, almost new and still in the original box, which is dried and cracked with age. Compared to his own HO set, the Lionel sure is big, and look at the dumb rail in the center of the track. Why would anybody build a train set like that?

Joey switches his attention to the opposite side of the trunk, where a large brown envelope has attracted his attention. Inside, he finds several funny-looking, black and white baseball cards. They look drab compared to the colorful cards of today, but at least he recognizes two of the players. One is Babe Ruth, the other, Joe DiMaggio.

Beneath the baseball cards are a couple of dozen 8 x 10 glossy photographs, all autographed. He instantly recognizes Clark Gable as Rhett Butler and John Wayne as the Ringo Kid, but who are those other people? Tom Mix? Stan Laurel and Oliver Hardy? Spencer Tracy? Clayton Moore? *Clayton Moore!* If only the kids back home could see what the Lone Ranger looked like without his mask! Maybe those other people were actually somebody, too. "Other people," like Errol Flynn, Bing Crosby, Betty Grable, Humphrey Bogart and Judy Garland, to name just a few.

Joey continues to sift through the trunk, finding little else of interest. When he looks at the ugly statuette of a bird in one corner, he wonders why either Grandma or Uncle Oscar would save such a monstrosity. He doesn't even notice that the bird looks exactly like the one in the picture with Humphrey Bogart.

His inspection complete, Joey closes the trunk and heads towards the stairs, not even glancing at the stack of yellow, brittle newspapers. If he had only sorted through them, he would have seen some *very* interesting headlines: "Lusitania Torpedoed;" "Lindbergh Lands in Paris;" "Amelia Earheart Declared Missing;" "Japs Bomb Pearl Harbor;" "Invasion;" "V-E Day;" and perhaps the most famous headline of all time, "Dewey Defeats Truman."

Joey can be forgiven for not recognizing the value of those old newspapers and some of the things in the trunk. After all, thousands of supposedly intelligent, sophisticated adults throw out perfectly good, *valuable* collector's items every day. The results are often disastrous, when compared to the money they could have made selling the stuff in the right marketplace.

Is everything that's old valuable? Certainly not. A lot of it *is* junk, especially if it's in poor condition. But a lot of things create a feeling of nostalgia, which Mr. Webster describes as "a wistful yearning for something past or irrecoverable." I have my own definition of nostalgia. I think it's a mental condition which makes us forget the bad things of the past and remember only the good.

An autographed picture of Tom Mix or an old Lionel train may not be able to bring back the carefree days of our youth, but they can bring back the best memories of those times. Most important of all, from a recycling point of view, is that millions of people are willing to pay good money for that pleasant stroll down Memory Lane.

Antiques & Collectibles

Who the heck was Hoyt Wilhem?

Well, it all depends on your point of view. To Ted Williams, he was that "#&*%~#* Wilhelm," one of the five toughest pitchers Williams ever faced. To the kid next door, Hoyt Wilhelm was a real nobody, only worth $50. At least, that's all his Topps baseball card for 1954 is worth, according to one guide. In another, he's worth even less, only $25. Williams, on the other hand, is worth $500. Yet a mere rookie outshines them both. Depending on condition, *his* card is worth $500 to $950. Of course, that rookie was Hank Aaron, the guy who finally broke Babe Ruth's home run record! Mickey Mantle outshines them all, he's worth a whopping $1,300. Find a 1952 card of the Mick, and you can up the ante to $7,500.

Any kid who is lucky enough to find an authentic, 1909 or 1910 Piedmont Tobacco card of Honus Wagner in *any* condition won't have to worry about financing his college education. That particular card is worth $50,000. Some collectors estimate a Honus Wagner card in near-mint condition would bring a cool half million.

What makes a player who is relatively unknown today worth so much more than "big names" like Aaron or Mantle? Obviously, scarcity, demand and condition all play their part in determining value.

Perhaps nowhere else in recycling is it more important to have a working knowledge of values than in antiques and collectibles. If you salvage a working, black and white TV and sell it for $10, then learn it is worth $25, it's no great disaster. There will probably be another like it just next week. But some items come along only once in a lifetime, and then only to the lucky few. How many people will get to own the jersey Babe Ruth wore in his last game? Obviously, only a handful in the next 100 years. (I had enough couth *not* to ask its owner what he had paid for it.) Selling that particular item for a mere $10 to $20 just because "it's an old baseball shirt" *would* be a disaster.

The key to knowledge, of course, is research. There are numerous price guides published for antiques and collectibles of all kinds. In some categories, such as sports cards and comic books, there are more than one. Prices for individual items may vary from one guide to another, but that doesn't necessarily mean one guide is good and the other worthless. The people who compile the guides do so with the information available to them, and *their* sources may not agree. After all, if a certain item has been selling for $100 for years, and one suddenly sells for $500 at auction, which is the most reliable indicator? Should the higher price be accepted as the new standard, or is it a fluke?

Regional differences in supply and demand, plus local economic conditions, are also reflected in prices. An item which might go begging for $25 in Chicago or Detroit could easily sell for far more in Dallas or Oklahoma City, and vice versa.

What's the difference between antiques and collectibles? Sometimes, there isn't any, although most antiques are collectible. Some collectibles, on the other hand, are definitely *not* antiques. Many of the most desirable collectibles are of fairly recent manufacture.

One definition of an antique is something that is more than 50 years old. Another is that it's an item which was made in a bygone era. But how do you define a bygone era? Is it pre-1900, pre-World War Two, or pre-Vietnam era? To stretch the point, it could be just last week. After all, that's gone just as surely as the days of the American Revolution or the apex of Egyptian glory. It just isn't as far removed.

Further confusion can be encountered when trying to decide whether something is a classic or an antique. The '57 Chevy is considered by many to be *the* classic car of the 1950s, yet it's hardly an antique. A 1930s Bugatti Royale, on the other hand, is not only an antique, but a highly collectible prize for anyone who can afford it. The last auction price I've seen on one of those was $8,500,000. Imagine buying insurance on that baby!

A set of *Star Trek* dinner plates is hardly an antique, nor are John Wayne or Elvis decanters, or a Roy Rogers wrist watch. Yet all are highly desirable collectors' items, commanding many times their original selling price.

For our purposes, we won't try to make a distinction between antiques and collectibles. Our concentration will be on the more practical aspects of them, such as buying and trading for them, then selling them at a profit.

While some antique shops carry just about any item that can legitimately qualify within that category, others specialize in antiquities, which are basically *much* older antiques. These include, but are not limited to, prehistoric Indian artifacts, Ming Dynasty vases, Egyptian sarcophagi, etc. Such items are very rare, very expensive, and often faked. The antiquities market is definitely *not* for amateurs, nor is it even suited for most professionals. It's mentioned here merely in passing, and should be left to the experts. Just about anyone who is reasonably intelligent, willing to work, and not afraid to do research can get into the antique business, however, even if it's only on a small scale to start.

Begin with one area of concentration and learn as much as you can about it. As your knowledge and experience increase, so will your inventory and sources of supply.

What should you choose? Obviously, it should be something that interests you. That will make your research, buying, and selling more fun, hence you will be more likely to become an expert at it. If your main field of interest is the Civil War, it will be hard to sustain an interest in Baroque musical instruments or the Spanish Inquisition year after year. A person who is fascinated with the Old West will be much happier selling old spurs, saddles and Indian artifacts than Victorian furniture or Depression-era glassware. Besides, even saddles are much lighter than Victorian furniture. The latter was solid wood, rather than particle board veneer, and was *very* heavy.

As with antiquities, there are fakes in antiques, and some of them are very good. Several years ago, I saw what appeared to be a very rare Colt Paterson revolver at a gun show. "Is that real, or a replica?" I asked the dealer who was exhibiting it. "It took a Colt expert several hours to determine that it's a very, very good fake," he replied. "He was only able to detect three minor errors in the copy job."

In another instance, I was examining what appeared to be a batch of "old" holsters similar to those used by cowboys and gunfighters in the 1880s. Even though I've done leather work for years, they certainly had me fooled. I only became suspicious when I realized the manufacturer's stamp on the holsters was identical to the logo on the dealer's business card. He freely admitted the holsters were of recent manufacture, and were purposely aged to make them *look* old. He wasn't trying to deceive anyone, but was merely catering to a small, select clientele. He had a valid concept, as many people who collect old handguns like to display them in holsters authentic to the era. Since the real thing is rare, expensive, and seldom encountered in good condition, he was offering them a practical alternative. Serious collectors would obviously be averse to displaying a pre-1900 Colt in a fast-draw rig, which is actually a design concept from the 1950s.

Of course, in some cases fakes are actually preferable to the authentic article. One Saturday afternoon, business was slow at the swap meet, so my wife decided to walk several nearby rows in search of anything we might be able to use. She returned in a few minutes and told me to go look at an old Plains Indian war bonnet which a yard saler was trying to sell. "It looks like it's probably the real thing, and he only wants sixty-five dollars for it," she said.

I followed her directions to that vendor's space, then casually looked at several items he had. Of course, my peripheral vision was always focused on the war bonnet. I went back to our setup and told my wife that I wouldn't even consider buying the War bonnet. "I have a sneaky suspicion those are real eagle feathers, not dyed turkey

feathers," I told her. End of argument. The mere possession of eagle feathers can lead to serious consequences
with Uncle Sam. The law does have special clauses covering museum exhibits and family heirlooms, but for the
average person, eagle feathers and claws are strictly *ver-
boten.*

Of course, we've also had to pass up some very good,
perfectly legal antique bargains a time or two. Once, we
could have bought an entire steamer trunk full of old
player piano rolls for a mere $5. We had to turn it down
because there was simply no room in our pickup to haul
it home. We knew we were making a mistake, but we had
no idea just how serious it was until weeks later. The
profit on those would easily have paid the grocery bill for
the next few weeks!

Just what are antiques worth? Obviously, some are
more valuable than others. Since I'm no expert on the
subject, I decided to visit the local antique mall to do a
little research. The mall is an interesting place, as it con-
sists of a number of small stalls rented to individual dealers. Some staff their stalls themselves, while others merely
allow customers to take their purchases to a central cash-
ier. There was a lot of stuff that I can't imagine anyone
wanting, but then everyone to their own taste.

I was, however, amazed at some of the prices I saw,
both for items that were true antiques and for a few that I
would seriously question as even being collectibles.

Of the few antiques that I really liked, the highlight
of the entire mall was a genuine Wells, Fargo & Co. stage
station mailbox, priced at $950. An old White rotary
sewing machine, which appeared to be in good working
order, bore a price tag of $60. That made me wonder

what ever became of my mother's old treadle Singer, which would undoubtedly be worth far more. Lionel train locomotives of fairly common type were priced at $110 to $200. A rare Lionel station from the 1930s was $2,000. A Toledo scale similar to the ones once found in meat markets was $250, while an old RC Cola outdoor thermometer carried a $38 price tag.

Interested in those *Star Trek* dinner plates I mentioned earlier? They were a mere $625, while a very unusual Scopitone 16mm juke box was priced at $7,900 firm. The spec sheet didn't say if it included sound films of Elvis singing "Heartbreak Hotel" or Bill Haley and the Comets rocking to "Rock Around The Clock," but they were from the appropriate era.

I'll have to admit there was one particular item near the entrance that raised my blood pressure and induced a severe case of mechanical lust. It was a magnificently restored 1937 V-12 Packard Boattail Roadster at a mere $275,000. I wonder if the owner would take one wife, three cats, a dozen or so guns and my collection of Roy Rogers comic books as a partial down payment? That is, of course, after I've had a chance to reread the latter.

Speaking of Roy Rogers, the local classical music station is playing "William Tell Overture" even as I write these words. If the title is unfamiliar, the music itself should certainly jar the memory of anyone born before about 1960. It's better known as the Lone Ranger's theme song. Thoughts of Roy Rogers and the Lone Ranger carry me back to those thrilling days of yesteryear, when we all rode the Happy Trails of childhood.

My lack of interest in antiques in general is more than made up for by a lifelong love for certain types of collectibles. At the top of the list are comic books, original comic strip drawings and anything related to the great cowboy stars of the B movie era. Come to think of it, I always thought Tarzan and Zorro were pretty neat, too.

Apparently I'm not alone in my fascination for the sagebrush heroes of the silver screen. One company has recently issued a limited edition Roy Rogers wrist watch, and there are several shops that specialize in movie cowboy memorabilia. To date, there have been at least three books published on the subject, with one devoted exclusively to Hopalong Cassidy. In glancing through it, I was amazed at the prices of certain Hoppy items. I may not be able to afford $450 for a Hoppy potato chip can, but at least I still have the lucky coin he gave me back in 1951.

For those who are too young to remember those days, Hoppy's first season on then-fledgling TV created a hero-worship phenomenon equivalent to Elvis's ascendancy to stardom a few years later. Hopalong Cassidy merchandise soon appeared in almost every store. Actor William Boyd couldn't even begin to meet the demand for personal appearances. He solved the problem by authorizing several look-alikes to fill in for him at rodeos, parades, etc.

The licensing of cowboy names and images on consumer goods dates back to the 1930s, with Buck Jones and comix leading the pack. "Upstarts" like Gene Autry and Roy Rogers soon joined in, for they and their business managers knew a good thing when they saw it. In fact, Gene Autry credited his licensees with supporting his wife in style while he went off to fight World War Two. "I made seventy thousand dollars as a singing cowboy in 1941," he recalled. "In 1942, I suddenly went to one hundred and forty dollars a month as an Army pilot. I'm still grateful to all those people who made the cap pistols, cowboy shirts and coloring books."

His sentiments were echoed by Fred Harman, creator of the popular *Red Ryder* comic strip. "I made far more money off the BB guns than I ever did from the comic strip," he said in the late 1960s. Of course, Red and his youthful Indian companion, Little Beaver, rode onto the silver screen shortly after the comic strip premiered in the late 1930s. Republic Pictures churned out a number of Red Ryder serials and feature films. These films are memorable mainly as the vehicles which introduced future cowboy stars Don "Red" Barry, "Wild Bill" Elliott and Alan "Rocky" Lane to movie audiences. Of course, there was also at least one Lone Ranger and several Zorro serials from Republic.

In addition to their own licensed products, the movie cowboys sold literally tons of cereal, candy bars, chewing gum and bread for their radio and TV sponsors. Both Hopalong Cassidy and the Lone Ranger appeared in a series of collectors' cards which were packaged in loaves of bread. A complete set of either in good condition is worth roughly $1,000 today. These giveaway premiums undoubtedly sold millions of dollars' worth of food products for the manufacturers. After all, what kid wouldn't insist that his mother buy Shredded Ralston or Ralston Cream of Wheat so he could get a Tom Mix secret decoder ring, telescope and treasure map? Pretty good merchandising, considering "Tom Mix" was a popular radio show many years after the star's death. I don't remember who played him on the radio, but it obviously wasn't Tom. His movie career essentially ended when talkies came in, as his squeaky voice was inconsistent with his heroic image.

All of the merchandise generated by these cowboys, plus a host of others, now falls into the collectible category. Numerous other hit TV shows also featured merchandising tie-ins ranging from plastic toys and lunch boxes to comic books.

As for comic books, they are among the most collectible of items, cowboy or otherwise. The first issue of *Superman* is worth an estimated $60,000 in near-mint condition. By contrast, the first Roy Rogers issue is worth a mere $50 to $350, depending on condition. Even John Wayne had a comic book series, with current prices in the same range as Roy's. If the John Wayne issue has art work by Frank Frazetta, the price goes up. Frazetta went from doing comic books to science fiction and fantasy paperback covers, calendars, etc., and became an extremely collectible artist in his own right. Today, his covers for the old Ace editions of Edgar Rice Burroughs' works are extremely collectible.

Needless to say, any early Disney items are also popular collectibles. The earliest Donald Duck comics are especially valuable. The name of writer/illustrator Carl Barks is almost synonymous with Donald, Daisy, Uncle Scrooge, etc. The Disney studio obviously appreciated the part Barks played in making the Duck comics a success. When he retired, they authorized him to do "fine art" oil paintings featuring the Duck family. These paintings sold for $20,000 to $40,000 during the 1970s, and only a few galleries were fortunate enough to get them.

There were a number of Disney toys on the market as early as 1934, when Mickey Mouse alone sold over

$34,000,000 worth of merchandise. Today, a Lionel Mickey Mouse hand car *ca.* 1940 is worth between $300 and $500. There were at least two versions of Goofy with a wheelbarrow, with the earliest being the most valuable. The 1930s edition is worth $400 to $700. The much more common 1960 version only brings $10-$20.

Topping the list in both scarcity and price for Disney items is original comic strip and animation art. Ever an innovator, Walt Disney made animation history in the late 1930s when he announced that he would make a feature-length animated cartoon of *Snow White.* Many skeptics predicted that would spell financial ruin for the Disney studio. They forgot who was making the picture! In addition to other innovations, Walt used *Snow White* to pioneer the use of the multi-plane animation camera. Prior to that time, animation was a rather crude process employing only two cels (short for celluloid) per movie frame. The top cel contained the action, while the bottom one was merely background. The multi-plane camera enabled the Disney artists to use multiple cels to create any number of special effects. It also set the standard for animation technique for years to come, until the advent of computerized animation in the 1980s.

Never one to ignore financial opportunities, Disney began selling old animation cels to collectors as early as the 1950s. At that time, run-of-the-mill cels from cartoon shorts sold for around $35. By the 1980s, the price had escalated to several hundred dollars for those same cels. "Choice" cels sold for considerably more, with some interesting contradictions. Although the lead character in *Snow White* was the girl of the same name, she was less in demand than the evil queen/witch. An action cel featuring the heroine was worth only about $3,000, while the witch commanded $5,000. A complete cel package (foreground, or action, middle and background) brought a considerably higher price. Sotheby's sold one especially desirable package featuring Snow White and the Prince for a record $209,000. That amount was equal to a significant percentage of the original production cost of the entire movie!

Of Disney comic strips, the most desirable originals are of Mickey Mouse by Ub Ewerks, *ca.* 1930-31. If any still exist, they are worth an estimated $10,000 to $50,000. Next on the list would be Ferd Gottfredson's 1933 drawings, at $1,200 each. For those done in 1970, the price drops to $150, with present-day originals only worth about $50 each.

Comic-strip collecting is a popular hobby in itself, albeit of limited appeal. Still, there is enough interest to warrant published price guides. The price for a given strip will vary from one daily to the next. Generally, the most valuable are those which show the main character at an important point in the story line. Releases featuring only secondary or minor characters are worth considerably less. Since several different artists might draw a strip over the years, that also influences the value. As an example, the *Tarzan* dailies by Harold Foster (of *Prince Valiant* fame) might command upwards of $1,000 each, while those by Russ Manning only bring $100 to $200. In my opinion, the Manning art is actually superior, but his originals aren't nearly as rare, hence collectible. By the same token, a *Batman* daily by strip creator Bob Kane is worth $1,500 as compared to $50 to $100 for present-day strips.

Most collectors consider Milton Caniff's *Terry & The Pirates* to be the ultimate adventure strip, with dailies selling for $300 to $600. Caniff left *Terry* to launch *Steve Canyon* in 1947, which he continued to draw until his death more than 40 years later. A *Steve Canyon* daily sells for $100 to $200.

Fred Harman's *Red Ryder* brings $200 to $400 from collectors, with 1960s dailies drawn by Bob MacLeod fetching considerably less. MacLeod drew the strip only a short time before abandoning it to pursue dual careers as a cowboy artist and Western novelist.

While none of the above strips are likely to turn up in thrift shops or at yard sales, a number of collectible items are. Old magazines, especially early issues of *Life, National Geographic, The Saturday Evening Post, Playboy*, etc., are highly collectible and can occasionally still be found at bargain prices. Not too long ago, a local book store had a copy of the December 8, 1941 issue of *Life*. It's interesting that the cover photo was of General Douglas MacArthur, supreme allied commander in the Pacific. That photo was also a bit prophetic, as the cover date was also the date the United States declared war on Japan. Despite its historical significance, that issue was priced at a mere $30.

Old cameras are swiftly gaining popularity with collectors, as are World War Two victory posters, old tobacco cans, etc. Of course, anything connected with the original 1939 release of *Gone With The Wind* is highly collectible, especially the movie tie-in paperback book, old lobby cards and movie posters, tickets to the original premier, etc.

As for that "ugly statuette of a bird" mentioned in the last chapter, that's a story in itself. Little Joey didn't find it, but it actually did turn up at a swap meet on the East Coast not too long ago. A movie buff thought it looked vaguely familiar and bought it for $8. As of this writing, there is some question as to its authenticity. If ultimately authenticated, it could potentially bring from $30,000 to $50,000 at auction. What makes it so valuable? It may very well be the central prop in the classic Humphrey Bogart movie, *The Maltese Falcon.*

Like gold, antique and collectible treasure is definitely where you find it!

Arts & Crafts From Junque

Government waste is always a sore point with taxpayers, and rightly so. After the usual categories of defense, foreign aid, welfare and roads that go nowhere, one of the favorite areas of criticism is expenditures for so-called "art."

Quite often, the controversy occurs immediately after the unveiling of a new sculpture on the lawn of a municipal or county building. Outraged citizens protest the fact that Pablo Pistachio was paid $42,000 to weld a toilet bowl, two old fenders and a bicycle frame together and christen it "Cosmic Destiny" or whatever. More often than not, the criticism is thoroughly justified.

One fact never seems to make the evening news. There are numerous artists and craftspeople who create *attractive*, and useful, items from unwanted trash and junk. Most sell their wares at craft shows and swap meets. A lucky few are actually featured in high-priced art galleries. For some, it's a way to supplement their retirement income. For others, it's actually a living. During the past couple of years I've met two or three who actually made a very good living recycling seemingly useless waste into arts and crafts.

Probably the single most common form of recycled arts and crafts is beer can biplanes. For those unfamiliar with them, they are exactly what the name implies: a miniature biplane constructed entirely from beer or pop cans. Although they've been around for years, they still attract a lot of attention at arts and crafts shows. Variations on the theme include sailing ships, windmills, and even steam locomotives or entire trains.

Frankly, beer can models are strictly a for-hobby-only proposition. They generally sell for $10 to $25, depending on size and detailing, and are very time-consuming to construct. There is simply no way a person can earn a living from them and still keep the price within reason. The people who *are* making money from these models are the ones who sell construction plans and instruction sheets. One fellow I know sells his for $3 per set. He doesn't sell a lot of them in a single day, but each sale usually takes less than a minute. If he sells out, he doesn't have to work day and night getting ready for the following week's show. He merely calls the printer and orders another 100 to 200 sets.

Somewhat similar, yet different, are egg carton sculptures. At least one enterprising artist in our area has developed a technique for creating humorous caricature sculptures from ordinary cardboard egg cartons. He uses the pre-formed egg receptacles to make the head and body parts, then cuts and folds the flat tops to form the arms and legs. His humans are hilarious characters based on occupations and avocations. They include doctors, nurses, firemen, carpenters, golfers and fishermen. He also does animals, with skunks, howling coyotes, flop-eared bunnies and frogs being the most popular. For those who want to try their hand at egg carton sculpture, he sells pre-cut kits for various figures. All the customer has to supply is glue, paint, and a pair of hands.

Last summer, my wife and I met a fellow who creates a different type of sculpture. We had seen him walking along a maintenance road the day before. He was picking up large pine tree limbs and pieces of small trunks the electric company had trimmed away from their power lines. Although it was in June, we assumed he was already gathering his winter firewood. Were we in for a surprise!

When we saw him at an arts and crafts show, we realized his specialty was carving animals from pine logs and the larger limbs. Although he had a variety of figures, his deer and javelina seemed to be the most popular. During the course of a two-day show, he sold 30 animals at an average price of $40 each. Not only did he put $1,200 in his pocket, he may have helped Smokey the Bear as well! If left along the maintenance road, all that scrap wood might well have become a fire hazard.

One of the most successful recycling people I know no longer recycles. He simply can't get enough used product to supply his needs. He began by making small shadow boxes from old yardsticks, then putting country miniatures on the shelves. These proved so popular that he finally had to start buying new yardsticks. He now orders them from the factory by the pickup load — and still has to order two or three times a year.

The list of arts and crafts which can be created from recycled objects is limited only by the human imagination. In the past year I've seen barnwood frames decorated with old barbed wire, Western sculptures made from horseshoes, jewelry from horseshoe nails, metal dachshunds with automobile spring bodies, penguins with shovel blade bodies, mirrors with horse collar frames, old railroad spikes with miniature pewter trains on them, etc.

One lady has a thriving mail order business with dried flower stationery kits. She presses flowers from her own garden in old telephone books donated by neighbors. She gets note paper and matching envelopes from a wholesale paper supplier and assembles everything into a kit, which is advertised in various craft magazines. She has customers in all 50 states, and has received numerous reorders from previous customers.

Her husband recycles discarded telephone line insulators into old-fashioned door latch knobs. Not to be outdone by this enterprising couple, a neighbor came up with yet another unique recycling craft. When the local post office moved into new quarters, he bought all the combination-lock doors from the P.O. boxes at the old location. He refurbished the locks, then installed the doors in small wooden boxes with a slot in the top. They are far more attractive than the average piggy bank, and far more secure. They sell very well at local arts and crafts shows.

Another fellow who is experienced at sheet metal work makes bird houses which are decorated to look like miniatures of real houses. He wasn't doing too well at the art show where we met him until a local Realtor came along. She ordered a large number to use as housewarming gifts for her clients. Her order totaled over $800, far more than he could have gotten for scrap sheet metal at the junk yard.

Although most artists and craftspeople sell their wares at swap meets or arts and crafts shows, some can produce enough to sell wholesale to stores and mail order houses. Their reasoning is that they are better off producing merchandise and selling it a little cheaper rather than paying high art show fees, sitting at the show all weekend, and maybe not selling anything.

While it's possible to increase gross sales drastically by wholesaling, it's not always the best way to go. The trick is to be able to sell at a wholesale price which allows stores to double it and still be able to sell the product. The wholesale price has to cover the cost of materials, plus a decent hourly wage for yourself. The latter should include time to gather materials, assemble the product, and deliver it to customers. If it has to be shipped, consider the time it takes to pack it and haul it to the post office or UPS terminal. If the product proves extremely popular, it may become impossible for one person to produce enough to meet the demand. Does the wholesale price allow you to hire help, pay them a decent wage, and still make a profit? How about an increase in the cost of supplies or materials? Can you absorb an increase, or must it be passed on to the customer?

These are all factors requiring considerable thought before making the decision to wholesale. When in doubt as to the answer on *any* factor, delay wholesaling until you have a satisfactory answer. The delay could prevent you from making some potentially lucrative sales, but it could also prevent you from working for zero profit, which is even worse.

Of course, it's possible to work for nothing selling retail at arts and crafts shows, or even lose money if sales are poor or the show is rained out. That risk can be minimized by picking only the *right* shows. This requires experience, knowledge and planning. A healthy dose of luck doesn't hurt, either.

First and foremost, your art or craft has to be something people will like — and buy. Comments on how clever you are or how much you're helping the ecology won't put food on the table. Sales are what counts. Even with the right product, sales won't automatically be good at every show. Factors which can influence sales include the size of the show, its location, attendance, the weather and the local economy, to name just a few.

Surprising as it may seem, one of the worst things that can happen to a beginning crafter is having a highly successful show the first time. One lady I know was ecstatic after working her first show. She had very little product, but still managed to gross $500 in sales. Since the show fee was only $10 and it was only a few minutes' drive from home, she felt flushed with success. For her next show, she increased her inventory drastically. The show fee was higher, and she had to travel 100 miles each way, necessitating an overnight stay in a motel. Her balloon of success burst when she grossed $23 for the entire weekend. There was nothing wrong with her product, she simply picked a bad show.

Although even the most experienced crafters can sometimes pick the wrong show, picking the good ones isn't as hard as it may seem. Talk to other artists and craftspeople. The more experienced ones generally have a regular show circuit they work. There may be some variation from year to year, but not much. They have learned from experience which shows are good and which are bad. The fact that a certain show is good for them doesn't guarantee that it will be good for you, but it's at least an indication.

Contrary to what it may seem, the show fee is really no indicator of sales potential. We have worked some low-priced shows which were very good, high-priced ones that were bad. In the latter case, the lucky exhibitors were the ones who actually made their show fee back — no profit, no travel expenses, they simply recouped their show fee.

As a basic rule of thumb, an exhibitor has to gross 10 times the show fee in order to make a show worthwhile. It's a rule of thumb *only*, but a good one. The lower the show fee, the higher the ratio must be to actually be profitable. The higher the show fee, the lower the ratio can be. This is especially true on very high-priced shows. One artist I know works a certain Las Vegas show every year. He has a large display, so his show fee is $4,000. On top of this, he has his travel costs, the cost of custom framing (expensive!), his materials, printing bills for his limited edition prints, etc. In round figures, let's assume these other expenses cost another $4,000, for a total of $8,000. A gross of 10 times the show fee would be $40,000. Does he take in that much? I doubt it, although it's possible. More than likely, he grosses somewhere between $15,000 and $20,000. That would give him a net profit of $7,000 to $12,000 for the show. Not bad for a three-day weekend!

When evaluating others' ratings for shows, consider the source. Some retirees who do arts and crafts as a hobby may be happy if they just recover their show fee and the cost of their materials. In other words, they're working to support their hobby, so may consider gross sales of $100 worthwhile. If they're trying to supplement their Social Security, the figure might increase to $200 to $300. A professional might consider $1,000 or more a poor gross, and rightly so. Anyone trying to make a living from the shows has to have consistently high gross in order to survive.

Sometimes a pro will work a mediocre show year after year simply because there aren't any good shows within a reasonable traveling distance that particular weekend. Occasionally, this will result in a pleasant surprise. Three years ago, we worked a mediocre show a few hours' drive from home simply because there was nothing else available. Sales were only fair, but we did make a small profit. The following year, our sales were even less. When show time arrived last year, we decided to give it one more try. "It's the only game in town," my wife explained as she looked at the calendar.

The third time was the charm. Our sales increased 50 percent over the preceding year, finally making the show worthwhile. Several other exhibitors also reported a significant increase in sales. An equal number said their sales were down from the preceding year. Which group did we believe? Both of them! Those who reported good sales were generally the ones who had a variety of merchandise and/or who had made some significant changes from the preceding year. Those who watched their sales decline were still doing the same old thing.

Take special note of the phrases "variety of merchandise" and "significant changes" in the preceding paragraph. They can often spell the difference between success and failure. This variety should include both *types* of merchandise and a wide range of prices. As of this writing, the country look is quite popular, with a lot of crafters doing variations on Holstein cows. To use them as an example, there will probably be very little demand for life-sized plywood silhouette Holsteins at $300 each. Wooden salt and pepper shakers painted in a Holstein pattern might sell very well, however, especially if priced at $2 to $5. Even in shows where high-priced items sell well, a variety of appealing items at less than $20 is essential. Quite often, such items may be all that sells at a show. Sell enough of them, and gross sales can be surprisingly high.

Remember, also, that the type of show can influence sales, as well as whether or not you will even be accepted. Some shows are limited to fine arts only, some to crafts only. The majority allow both. A few shows will, quite frankly, let in anyone who pays the show fee, regardless of what they sell. This doesn't necessarily mean those particular shows are bad. We've worked one such show every Labor Day weekend for years, and wouldn't even consider going anywhere else. Its official title is "Native American Cultural Fair and Swap Meet," which is slightly misleading. There is very little Native American culture there, but a lot of swap meet. I would estimate that at least 80 percent of the vendors who work that show are perpetual returnees, and with good reason. Whether selling arts and crafts or swap meet items, they consistently enjoy good sales. Invariably, when I ask one vendor how he did at the end of the day, his reply is, "This is Willow Canyon." What he's actually saying is, "Dumb question. Of course I had a good day."

Unless there is a steady influx of tourist traffic, try to avoid doing too many shows in one area which has a small population base. Local people can only support so many arts and crafts shows, both in attendance and purchases. The fellow who sold 40 pine log animals at one show made the mistake of doing another show at the same location just three weeks later. At the second show, he only sold three items. Other crafters who worked both shows reported equally disappointing sales the second time around. If you have no choice but to return to a certain, non-tourist area within a short time, hit them with something new each time. Variety is the spice of life — and sales.

Occasionally, a show will be worthwhile despite the fact everything is seemingly against it. When our scheduled Fourth of July weekend show was canceled a couple of years ago, we had to find a replacement rather quickly. The only show that wasn't full was a small one, in the parking lot of a general store in a fairly remote area. When we arrived at the show site, we found the promoter had neglected to mention one minor detail. The store had been closed for years. To add insult to injury, a dangerous killer had escaped from the state prison and was known to be hiding somewhere in the vicinity of the show site. "It's too late to go anywhere else," I told my wife as we viewed the weed-choked show area. "We might as well set up here and hope for the best."

Several other exhibitors looked the show site over and left, but enough stayed to form the nucleus of a halfway decent show. Although there was very little traffic the entire weekend (thanks mainly to Public Enemy Number One), almost every car that drove by stopped. When the occupants left the show, a very high percentage were carrying packages from one exhibitor or another.

On Saturday night, we learned the escaped killer had run a police roadblock and crashed his stolen pickup only six miles from the show site just a few hours earlier. "He realizes the cops know he's familiar with this area, so I bet he runs in the opposite direction," I predicted. As it turned out, I was right. He was captured nearly 30 miles away on Sunday morning.

At the end of the show, most exhibitors agreed their sales had only been about half what they hoped. But for the size of the crowd, they had been better than expected. All agreed the weekend had actually been fun, escaped killer and all. Too bad that little show is a thing of the past.

Most shows organized by professional promoters are run in an efficient and orderly manner. Surprisingly, not all are expensive, although many are. Smaller shows with non-profit or strictly local sponsors may be thoroughly disorganized events which just sort of happen. They may be fairly successful for awhile, then they fizzle and fall apart.

As an example of the latter type, consider the following example:

The Ladies Auxiliary for the Royal Order of the Mongoose, Lodge No. 432, decides they need a fund-raiser. It's late summer, with the local watermelon crop ready for harvest, so the Chamber of Commerce's annual Watermelon Daze celebration is only a month away. Since several of the ladies in the auxiliary do handicrafts, they decide to have an arts and crafts sale on the same weekend.

A show chairwoman is selected, and she arranges for the use of the lawn in front of the county library. The show isn't advertised, but a dozen or so members of the auxiliary each pay the $10 show fee and set up their displays on Saturday morning. The show is the first ever in the area, so several exhibitors do well. They repeat the show the following year, with the same results.

The third year, the show chairwoman decides they can raise more money if they increase the fee and open the show to outsiders. They raise the fee to $20 and mail press releases to area newspapers and several regional show guides.

Since there are only a couple of other shows anywhere in the state that weekend, approximately 50 outside exhibitors show up on Saturday morning. As happens at most shows, some do very well while others do poorly. Sales for most fall somewhere in between.

When the chairwoman totals up the exhibitors' fees, she is well aware of what the bank deposit will be on Monday morning. "We made a lot of money for the club this year," she comments to the club treasurer. "There's still plenty of space on the library lawn, so let's double the size of the show next year." The treasurer likes the idea, and suggests it at the next executive council meeting. Show expansion is unanimously approved.

A new show chairwoman is named. Unfortunately, she's long on enthusiasm and personality but short on follow-through and organizational ability. When show time arrives, there are 100 exhibitors to fill the spaces. The show layout is a hodgepodge, with a poor traffic flow pattern. Attendance is off due to lack of local advertising and promotion. Even worse, those who do attend are mostly local retirees with little disposable income. With only X number of potential sales dollars, the increased size of the show reduces everyone's sales potential. Needless to say, none of the exhibitors are happy at the end of the show. A few will try again, just in case this is an off year, but the number will decline each year. Ultimately, the show will die a natural death.

Although word of mouth is the best source of good shows, it isn't the only one. Each state has a tourist bureau which generally has a listing of all major events for the calendar year. Local Chambers of Commerce are also good sources of information on upcoming events in a specific area, or even statewide. Recently, we were returning home from a buying trip to the Navajo reservation in Northern New Mexico. As we drove through downtown Gallup, I noticed the Chamber of Commerce building just ahead. I pulled into the parking lot and we went inside. Five minutes later, we were back on the road. My wife was already perusing a current copy of *New Mexico Vacation Guide*. This activity was hardly new to her, as we always try to have guides for all the Southwest states in our files.

In addition to government-sponsored guides for most states, there are also a number of private publications devoted entirely to arts and crafts shows, fairs, etc. While some are too general in their information, others are very detailed. Many will send a potential subscriber a free sample, or will charge only a nominal fee for one. Some even distribute back issues free of charge at larger shows. Comparing several will help you decide which ones best suit your individual needs. Remember, the more specific the information, the better.

Although there are undoubtedly some excellent guides in other parts of the country, I'm only familiar with those which pertain to California, the Southwest and the Southeast. None lists every single show in the area covered. This isn't due to negligence on the editors' part, but rather a lack of communication from show organizers. After all, the guides can only list shows they know about. In some cases, shows are so specialized or limited in exhibitor space that they don't *want* to be listed. These shows are analogous to really good job openings. The best ones are never advertised. The two show guides we subscribe to are:

Hands On Guide, 255 Cranston Crest, Escondido, California 92025-7037, telephone (619) 747-8206. (Lists a wide variety of show types in California, the Southwest, Pacific Northwest and Wisconsin.)

ShoWhat, P.O. Box 6278, Phoenix, Arizona 85005-6278, telephone (602) 954-5169. (Limited to shows in Arizona, but the editor gladly shares information with subscribers on the few out-of-state shows he works. *ShoWhat* is especially valuable for its no-holds-barred reviews of previous shows.)

The third show guide of which I am aware that contains reviews is:

Sunshine Artist, 1736 County Road 427N, Longwood, Florida 32750-3410, telephone (407) 332-4944. (Covers a number of states in addition to Florida. While the reviews aren't as detailed as those in ShoWhat, they're still worthwhile.)

I have purposely avoided listing subscription rates as they are subject to change. A telephone call to any of the publications listed will get you the current rate. Each is well worth the price. After all, if you get just *one* good show from any of them, that show will pay for a year's subscription many times over.

What do you look for in a show? Obviously, good sales are your primary concern. If a show isn't reviewed in the guides, talk to artists who have worked it in the past. Try to get more than one evaluation. If you can't find anyone who has worked a particular show, try to read between the lines in the show listing. To illustrate how this is done, let's look at some hypothetical listings. Each show is based on one my wife and I worked within a one-month period, and only the names, locations and dates have been changed. My own between-the-lines evaluation is in parentheses following each listing. While my comments may be overly simplistic, they do give a rough indication of what to expect.

24th Annual Mother Lode Days, Aug. 7-8, Prospector Park, 1234 Main Street, Buzzard's Roost. Fine arts and crafts only, no swap meet items. 10x10 space, $15. A few larger spaces, $20. Contact Jim Hill, Buzzard's Roost Chamber of Commerce, 3456 Main Street, Buzzard's Roost, NV 98765, (678) 987-6543. (Check this one out on a state map or road atlas. Buzzard's Roost has a population of only 750, and it's the largest town within 100 miles. If you will just happen to be in the area at the time, it *might* be worth a try. Don't count on making travel expenses plus a profit on this one.)

First Annual Mother's Day Show, May 5-8, Dollar-Mart parking lot, Central City. Arts & crafts, jewelry, hand decorated clothing, antiques & collectibles. 20x20 space, $40; 30x40 space, $80. Contact Ray Swanson, 5678 Cedar, Pleasantville, UT 87654, (567) 345-6789. (A first-time show, so who knows? Fee is reasonable for space size, length of show. Could be good

Mother's Day gift sales, but don't expect much on Mother's Day itself. If Ray Swanson has a reputation for producing good shows, this one might be a winner.)

Rootin' Tootin' Wild West Days, April 27-30, Six-Gun Resort and Casino, Yucca City. Fine arts & handcrafted items by exhibitor only. 10x10 space on River Walk, $100. 15 spaces, returning vendors have priority. Juried by 4 photos, 2 of work, 1 of display, 1 of exhibitor in workshop or studio. Contact Gary Porterhouse, Marketing Div., Six-Gun Resort and Casino, 2345 Keno Dr., Yucca City, NV 87554, (678) 345-6789. Deadline March 1st. (A reasonably high show fee, but this one could be worth it. People at gambling resorts tend to buy after winning, or even before playing. Motel rooms and meals are cheap in Yucca City, which is a mini-Las Vegas. Early deadline indicates this show fills up *fast*, as does preference for returning vendors.)

While the examples above give a general idea of what to look for, there are other indicators which may not be as apparent. In general, art shows do poorly at events where there is an admission fee or a lot of entertainment. Remember: *when the entertainment starts, the buying stops.* Certain types of events also tend to attract the wrong type of crowd for arts and crafts sales. Rock and country music jamborees are prime examples. People go to drink beer and listen to the music, not to buy art.

As further examples of how to evaluate shows, let's look at some hypothetical reviews for the Buzzard's Roost, Central City and Yucca City shows, exactly as they might appear in *ShoWhat*. My own comments appear in parentheses.

24th Annual Mother Lode Days, Buzzard's Roost, Aug. 7-8. Of 5 artists reporting, none did well. After expenses, 2 went home with less money in their pockets than they came with. Show poorly laid out, too far from center of activities. Foot traffic extremely low at show, poor attendance at all activities despite perfect weather. Of 30 exhibitors on Sat., only 7 set up on Sun. None reporting would return. (Give this one a miss unless you live in Buzzard's Roost. Even then, you might be further ahead staying home and watching TV.)

First Annual Mother's Day Show, May 5-8, Dollar-Mart parking lot, Central City. Of 5 reporting, 2 did poorly, 3 reported sales over a grand. All felt weather affected sales. Windy Thurs., Fri., cold & rainy Sun. All said sales fair to good Sat. Excellent cooperation from Dollar-Mart manager. While not as good as Swanson's Memorial Day show at Watson Field, all reporting felt show has potential. Those with variety of merchandise, large displays did best. All would return. (Note all felt sales would have been better if the weather had cooperated, all would return. This show definitely deserves a second chance, and maybe even a third.)

Rootin' Tootin' Wild West Days, April 27-30, Six-Gun Resort and Casino, Yucca City. This show continues to be one of the best spring shows in the area. New applicants continue to outnumber total spaces available, with returning vendors always having priority. Few fail to return. A great show for those lucky enough to be accepted. (I won't even give *ShoWhat* a review on this one. The fewer people who know about it, the better. If your art or craft is truly unique and of outstanding quality, go ahead and apply. A miracle might happen and give you a chance to join the Chosen Few. Believe me, it beats having a terminally ill uncle with an oil well.)

As the bottom line, try to realistically evaluate your own sales potential at any given show before applying for it. I've seen a couple of exhibitors do poorly at the Six-Gun shows because they had the wrong merchandise. Remember, the promoter's job for any show is to provide a location and attract a crowd of potential buyers. Actual sales are up to you.

I have one final word of advice about planning shows: Buy a weekly planning calendar and use it. Most successful show exhibitors plan their schedule months in advance. By referring to last year's calendar, my wife can tell which weekends of each month we have a show scheduled and which ones we're free. That gives her plenty of time to look for good shows to fill in the blanks. Shows may be canceled at the last minute, of course, but at least we have some idea where we will be next month or six months from now. We also know when the lean times will be so we can stock the freezer with people food and the pantry with cat food. If there's anything noisier than a rumbling stomach, it's a hungry cat!

Military Surplus

With the collapse of the Soviet empire and the attendant dissolution of the Cold War, the military surplus market is in a state of flux. It may grow rapidly in the next few years or it may decline. Only one thing is certain. It will still be around.

Military surplus disposal in one form or another has been a problem for centuries if not thousands of years. After all, what did the barbarians do with all the swords, shields, helmets and breastplates they acquired when they sacked Rome? What became of the flint and stone weapons of the Aztecs, Incas and Mayans when Spain conquered those civilizations? What became of the catapults and siege machines after cannons were invented? What does the modern military do with obsolete weapons and materiel when it no longer needs them?

An early example of obsolete weapons disposal which resulted in scandal occurred shortly after the outbreak of the Civil War. In mid-1861, the government sold 5,000 obsolete Model 1843 Hall smoothbore carbines to a New Hampshire entrepreneur for $3.50 each. He then resold them to New York City gunsmith Simon Stevens. Stevens rechambered the guns, rifled the barrels, and sold them back to the government for $22 each. A Congressional investigation was launched, but those who profited from the transaction were quickly exonerated. Testimony revealed that the New Hampshire entrepreneur had originally offered to perform the same modifications at a cost of $1 per weapon, while they were still U.S. government property. In a typical display of bureaucratic bungling, the government had refused an offer that could have saved it thousands of dollars.

When the war ended, Northern carpetbaggers promised the newly-freed slaves each 40 acres and a mule. The government promised recently-discharged veterans nothing but a return to civilian life in a recession-plagued economy. Jobs were scarce in the East, so former Yanks and Johnny Rebs alike turned to the West to seek their fortunes. Thousands of surplus and "liberated" Civil War weapons went West with them. Foodstuffs were another matter. Civil War issue hardtack went into storage, to be· issued to troops in the field as late as the Spanish-American War of 1898.

Military surplus sales first became a large, nationwide industry in its own right shortly after World War Two. Literally billions of dollars' worth of surplus items were sold at auction in an attempt to recoup at least a part of their wartime cost. Thousands of tanks, ships and aircraft were stripped of all useable hardware and sold as scrap metal. Smaller items suitable for individual use found their way into a growing number of surplus stores, where they were resold to the public. These items included everything from safety razors and fleece-lined flight jackets (now a valued collectors' item) to sleeping bags and combat boots.

Civilian customers bought military surplus items for two reasons. First, they were of excellent quality. Second, they were invariably cheap, at least back then. Even as recently as the late 1960s, surplus small arms were selling at bargain prices. When deer season rolled around, thousands of hunters took to the field with surplus Springfields, Enfields and Mausers purchased for less than $20 each just a few weeks before. Today, any of those rifles in good condition is worth many times that price.

As the supply of GI-issue canteens, mess kits, web gear and ammo pouches began to dwindle, many surplus stores began selling imitations of current manufacture. Some were merely that, imitations, while others were billed as "military spec." In other words, they were supposedly produced to military specifications, but weren't actually GI-issue. Some customers willingly purchased the newer items. Other insisted on the genuine article.

Initially, the surplus store's main customers were hunters and campers. Why pay high prices for commercial camping gear when Charlie's Surplus City was jam-packed with GI-issue tents, canteens and backpacks at bargain prices? "Economically disadvantaged" people hadn't been invented yet, but there were a lot of poor Americans who bought surplus clothing simply because that was what they could afford. In the decades following World War Two, there have been several periods when the military look was "in" and people bought surplus clothing simply because it was trendy. A Vietnam-era flower child wearing cammies may seem incongruous, but many of them did.

When the Free World learned the Soviet Union had the atomic bomb in 1949, a new movement was born. Many Americans built fall-out shelters and stocked them with surplus C rations and jerry cans filled with water. They didn't know it at the time, but they were the forerunners of today's survivalists. Even today, some people view survivalists as lunatics who run around in cammies and stockpile thousands of rounds of ammunition for their favorite assault-type weapons. In reality, most survivalists are actually solid citizens who simply realize that a major disaster, natural or otherwise, *can* happen. They are far more likely to have a supply of food, blankets, candles and water in the trunk of their car than a fall-out meter and tripod-mounted machine gun.

Recognizing the needs of the true survivalist movement, several enterprising surplus stores in Southern California sell earthquake kits. These are simply backpacks filled with enough emergency supplies to see a person safely through the first two or three days following a major earthquake. A lot of residents of the Los Angeles area probably laughed at such kits prior to January 1994. They weren't laughing after the big rumble, especially when they started pricing staples at certain convenience markets in areas which suffered a lesser degree of damage.

Lest anyone think military surplus today is nothing but camouflage clothing, canteens, MREs (meals ready to eat), earthquake kits and World War Two-era gun parts, it isn't. It includes such diverse items as office equipment, X-ray machines and station wagons. Despite the general decline of availability in recent years, it's still possible at this writing to buy surplus items direct at government auction.

For information on military surplus auctions, simply call the main switchboard at the nearest military base. Ask the operator to transfer your call to the Department of Defense auction building. Simply state that you are interested in attending the next auction, and ask to be put on their mailing list.

If there is no military installation near you, or it doesn't conduct auctions, don't despair. There are numerous companies that specialize in wholesale surplus sales. Many exhibit at trade shows sponsored by Associated Surplus Dealers. These are *big* shows, and feature just about any type of general merchandise imaginable in nearly 5,000 booths. Several shows are held each year, with the most common locations being Las Vegas, Reno, and Atlantic City. For a current show schedule, contact:

Associated Surplus Dealers
2525 Ocean Park Boulevard
Santa Monica, CA 90405-5201

They also publish ASD/AMD Trade News, a large-format trade paper with a monthly circulation of nearly 90,000. It is mailed free to anyone who has registered at an ASD/AMD trade show within the preceding five years. In addition to numerous articles of interest to re-tailers, the publication features a variety of wholesale advertising, including some of the largest and most reputable surplus wholesalers.

Wholesale surplus ads can also be found in several specialty publications such as *East/West Coast Merchandiser*, etc. These are usually available free of charge at the office of most larger swap meets, and some of the better small ones.

Exploiting The News

Today's major news event may become tomorrow's forgotten trivia, but it can sometimes generate potentially good, short-term sales. All it takes is a quick wit, the boldness to be different, and timing. The latter is all-important. You have to act fast, before the major event is overshadowed by an even more significant one. The first guy on the bandwagon is also the most likely to succeed. Remember, selling is a monkey see, monkey do business. In other words, the first monkey has to reach the top of the banana tree before it collapses from the weight of all the other monkeys trying to climb it. It *will* eventually collapse, although the first monkey will get the choicest bananas.

The first example of a timely, waste-based entrepreneurial windfall of which I'm aware occurred in the early 1980s. Within days of the eruption of Mount St. Helens, a resident of the area was packaging volcanic ash in apothecary jars and selling them nationwide as souvenirs. They sold very well at the time, but doubtless would arouse little interest today.

When East Germany announced the Berlin wall would be torn down, world leaders hailed it is a great step toward international peace. At least one fellow saw the event in different light. To him, it was a golden opportunity to make money. He flew to Berlin, where he was photographed in front of the graffiti-littered wall. Once the demolition crews had completed their job, he gathered up pieces from the section against which he had been photographed. He crated the pieces and had them shipped to the United States, then broke them down into smaller pieces. He sold these at various swap meets, complete with a certificate of authenticity and a photo of himself standing next to the wall. Although his shipping bill was astronomical due to the weight, the product itself cost him nothing. When all was said and done, he had realized a nice profit from the endeavor.

The January, 1994 L.A. earthquake was a disaster for many in the area, a highly profitable windfall for others. The post-quake aftershocks were yet in the future when souvenir hunters began scrounging through the ruined homes of the rich and famous. Unlike most, Sam's scrounging was with profit in mind. He duly recorded the locations of some of his choicest finds in a notebook, then hauled them home and went to work. He framed various pieces of debris and offered them for sale at thoroughly ridiculous prices. Pieces of a broken bottle from the home of such and such movie star sold for $250 while a broken lamp from the home of another brought $350, etc. Amazingly, or maybe not too surprisingly, Sam had sold all of his salvaged treasures within a few days.

A fellow vendor at the local swap meet turned the earthquake to his advantage in a slightly different way. He was already planning a buying trip to L.A. when he heard about the earthquake, so he was in a position to act quickly. Realizing the long distance lines into the area would be overloaded, he simply waited until the next day to call his major supplier. After appropriate inquiries regarding the safety of the supplier's family, home, business, etc., Wallace got right to the point. "Do you have anything that was damaged in the quake that might be salvageable?" he asked.

"We've got quite a few items that received minor to a fair amount of damage, but weren't actually destroyed," the supplier answered. "In fact, the insurance adjuster has already been here and we've agreed on a settlement. [The supplier was a *big* policyholder, who rated fast action.] The warehouse crew is clearing the stuff out now."

"Tell them to stop, or to work *real* slow," Wallace said. "I'll be at your place first thing in the morning."

Wallace drove half the night, but he was waiting at the warehouse when they opened for business the next day. After loading his regular order onto his truck, he backed it up to the second loading dock where the damaged goods were stacked. He added them to his load, then commenced the long trip home.

When he opened the boxes of damaged goods the next day, he found carousel music boxes with broken horses, porcelain dolls with broken or mangled arms or legs, etc. At that point, most people would have thrown the stuff away, but most people don't think like Wallace. The following Saturday, a special table in his swap meet setup bore the following sign:

EARTHQUAKE SPECIAL
Damaged goods direct from L.A.!
$1.00 each or 6 for $5.00

Believe it or not, people actually stood in line to buy Wallace's earthquake specials. By the end of the day, he had sold $180 worth. He sold even more the following day, and still had quite a few items left.

While Wallace obviously didn't make a fortune selling earthquake specials, he did sell enough to pay all the travel expenses for a trip he would have taken anyway. The following weekend, he didn't bother to put the rest of his damaged goods on display. He simply waited a couple of weeks, then sold them at an aftershock sale!

Of course, it isn't really necessary to wait for an earthquake or other disaster to get free merchandise. There are plenty of saleable items which the average person would never think of as potential money. As an example, who would buy dirt? Not several tons of fill dirt for construction purposes, but a plain little jar of dirt? The answer is: enough people to make collecting it worthwhile, provided it's from the right area.

Within the last few years, there has been a resurgence of nostalgic interest in the old Route 66 which once linked Chicago with L.A. Virtually every tourist trap and even many chain stores along present-day Interstate 40 now display Route 66 souvenirs of every conceivable description. One of the more unusual items is small apothecary jars filled with dirt from the original Route 66 roadbed. Although Route 66 may not have inspired international headlines or captured the feature spot on the 10:00 o'clock news, it's obviously a very marketable piece of American history.

Of course, a guy could get into big trouble trying to sell pieces chipped from the wall of the Alamo, or dirt from the Custer battlefield, but there are other possibilities. With a bucket and a *very* long rope, how about sea water from inside the *Titanic*? If that idea seems all wet, how about a piece of cloth cut from the wedding dress of the widow of the Unknown Soldier?

Wallace's Secret

When Wallace first began selling, he realized that he would have to stand out from the crowd if he was going to be successful. He looked himself straight in the mirror and asked, "What makes me different from anyone else?" He didn't mean his physical characteristics. What he meant was his experience, attitude, knowledge, and general thinking patterns. In actuality, he was saying, "It's a tough world out there. What edge do I have over the other guy?"

Wallace pondered the problem for a while, then realized that he already knew the actual secret of successful selling. It was so simple, he wondered why it wasn't universally known. In any sales presentation, the worst that can happen is the customer will say "no." Think about it a moment. Is that really so bad? After all, the customer can also say "yes," and often does.

Wallace applied his new-found knowledge at the swap meet. His enthusiasm and optimism paid off, and his sales increased. Flushed with success, he decided to explore new territory.

Of course, Wallace's merchandise was a big plus when he decided to branch out. He has a steady source of supply for discontinued, overstocked and slightly damaged gift items, at mere pennies on the wholesale dollar. The former he simply sells at prices well below those found in stores, yet his profit margin is much higher. The latter he repairs and enhances, so the final product is actually different from what the stores sell. As a result, he has one of the classiest and most successful small recycling businesses imaginable. (His enhancement also qualifies him for certain art shows, which permit exhibitor-enhanced commercial items.)

Wallace approached numerous civic groups, clubs and churches about doing special shows for them. "How would you like to make money for your organization, with no investment of any kind and very little work on your part?" became one of his most successful opening lines. Naturally, any non-profit organization is always interested in raising money, especially without expending any extra effort. Once he had their attention, Wallace would hit them with Line B: "I can sell top quality gift items for 50 to 70 percent below stores, give your organization 25 percent right off the top, and still make a profit. Are you interested?" Some said "no," but a high percentage said "yes." In fact, Wallace was so successful at promoting his specialty shows that he even did one for a regional office of the IRS! Of course, they got their percentage the following April 15th.

Believe it or not, Wallace's biggest success has actually been selling through banks. Sure, banks are in the business of lending money, not retail sales, but that doesn't mean they totally reject the idea of the latter.

Wallace began by approaching the manager at the branch where he did his own banking. When the manager politely but firmly stated that banks aren't in the retail business, Wallace beefed up his sales approach. "Aren't you interested in community good will?" he asked. "Wouldn't you like to sponsor a Little League team, or make a generous donation to the Community Chest, without it costing the bank a dime?"

The manager finally capitulated, and allowed Wallace to put a small display in an unused showcase in one corner of the bank lobby. Two days later, he called Wallace and said, "Come put some more stuff in the case."

"You mean you've sold some already?" Wallace asked, feigning surprise. The case is empty," the manager explained. "My own tellers bought it all."

Wallace restocked the case later that afternoon, and he had to restock it again the following Monday. Word soon got around among the various branch managers. Before long, Wallace had displays in every branch office in a large metropolitan area. He soon gave up working the swap meet altogether on Fridays. Instead, he used that day to service the banks. Of course, it was no coincidence that he picked the day which was payday for most people. "Why should I work the swap meet on Friday, when it might be slow or a rain-out?" he asked. "I can make six or seven hundred, guaranteed, just restocking the banks."

Although most of his merchandise is in the $20 to $50 price range, he occasionally sells larger pieces (up to $400 each) in his bank displays. His best sales are from mid-April through early May and October through mid-December, when people are buying Mother's Day or Christmas gifts. Since most people either have money in their pockets when they enter the bank or come out, why shouldn't they do their gift shopping there? It saves them an extra stop.

Last October, one branch alone sold over 400 carousel horses for Wallace. It isn't unusual for a new branch to sell 75 percent of its initial display within the first three days. Quite often, the bank's tellers and other employees are Wallace's first customers.

Wallace doesn't even have to take care of the receipts. The banks automatically credit his share of the gross to his account, which once led to an interesting encounter with the manager of the RV resort where he was living. As she distributed the tenants' mail, she noticed an unusual number of bank envelopes going into Wallace's box. Concerned about a good tenant's possible financial problems, she asked him if anything was wrong. Wallace tore open one of the envelopes and waved the contents under her nose. "Trouble?" he asked. "These aren't dunning notices, they're deposit slips!"

The Ultimate Recycling: Restoration

How do you explain to your wife of many years that you've fallen hopelessly in love? It happened to me while researching this chapter, as it's happened to thousands of others my age or a little older. In many cases, the wife actually realized she was the second love even before she said, "I do."

Fortunately, my wife was as understanding as the other ladies when I explained the facts. My new love isn't another woman, although the pinup girl who graces her nose is certainly appealing. Her name is *Sentimental Journey*, and she's the most completely and accurately restored B-17G heavy bomber to be found anywhere in the world.

As I gazed fondly at the 50 year old beauty for the first time, I could almost hear the pilots groan as the briefing officer said, "Target for today... Berlin." I could easily imagine the roar of the mighty Wright Cyclones as hundreds of heavily-laden planes lumbered down the fog-shrouded runways and lifted into the cold, pre-dawn darkness. It took little more imagination to see the flak exploding over the target area, the German fighters boring in for the kill, focusing their attention on the cripples. I could almost feel the anxiety of the crews as they sweated out the return flight. Short on fuel, with two engines out, wounded aboard and heavy flak damage, could they possibly reach England? Back at the base, the ground crews waited anxiously. They paced the wet tarmac, smoked innumerable cigarettes, listened for the sound of the mighty engines. Would *their* ship, *their* crew return?

What makes an old, obsolete bomber so appealing? Why does the mere sight of one conjure up images like those described above? Nostalgia is certainly a major factor. As for the rest, it's like riding a Harley. Attempts to explain it are futile. People either understand, or they don't. The bottom line is that old airplanes, especially warbirds, are appealing, rare, and expensive.

Although the greatest warbird interest is in combat-type aircraft, trainers are also popular and becoming more so all the time. The reason is simple. Far more trainers survived the war and postwar demilitarization, therefore they are more plentiful and affordable. As an example, an AT-6 Texan advanced trainer in good condition currently sells for about $150,000. A prime example might bring $200,000. Virtually *any* type of World War Two fighter in good condition will easily bring $500,000. The same plane, in pieces on the hangar floor, will still cost $300,000 or *more* to restore.

Regardless of type, the available supply of warbirds will never again be able to meet the demand. Natural attrition will only intensify the situation. Every year, one or two crash on the air show or racing circuit. Some can be salvaged, but most are written off. The highly modified F4U Corsair that crashed during the Phoenix 500 air race in the spring of 1994 will serve as an example. The pilot survived. The plane, which was valued at over $1,000,000, was a total loss. In 1959, the airframe alone might have been purchased for as little as $150. Today, it would easily be worth $200,000 or more.

As late as 1959, there was no shortage of bare airframes or restorable aircraft from the World War Two or the Korean War eras. Litchfield Naval Air Facility, just outside Phoenix, had over 5,000 planes in storage. A Corsair airframe could be had for as little as $150, as mentioned earlier. Just beyond a row of derelict fighters, the crushers were pounding other now equally rare warbirds into unrecognizable cubes of metal.

Even in the early 1960s, numerous Mustangs, B-25 Mitchell bombers and AT-6 Texans in various states of disrepair languished in the back corners of numerous small airports.

As the postwar years flew by, a curious thing happened. The fresh-faced kids who had flown those planes against the Axis became old men, or at least middle-aged. Forgotten were most of the horrors of war. They remembered the good buddies, the safe returns from tough missions, the elation or sense of relief when they first heard the war was over. Instead of scanning the skies for a returning group or squadron members, they now gazed wistfully upward, just hoping to glimpse a warbird in flight.

It may have been an attempt to recapture lost youth. Perhaps it was a natural outgrowth of nostalgia. For whatever reason, many veteran pilots began displaying serious interest in restoring and flying wartime aircraft — if they could find them.

By 1957, not one of the 15,000 P-47 Thunderbolts built during the war was still flying in the U.S. Airframes could still be found in fairly abundant quantities, but a complete, flyable airplane? Forget it! A number of larger aircraft suitable for firefighting were still flying, but there was hardly a glut of World War Two aircraft on the market.

With demand suddenly exceeding supply, a new industry was born. Several small companies began specializing in rebuilding and restoring vintage aircraft. While this may well be the ultimate form of recycling, it isn't easy. Those who do it must be as much bloodhound and detective as mechanic. They have to ferret out original parts wherever they can. A B-17 top turret might be found in a hayloft in Iowa, in use as a skylight in a restaurant in Nevada, or as an oversized planter in a sun room in Florida. If a restorer can't find original parts, and often he can't, he will have to make new ones. This requires access to original factory blueprints, which may no longer exist, or precise measurement of an existing part. Needless to say, extensive and expensive machining and sheet metal fabricating facilities are required. It's simply not possible to rebuild a warbird with little more than a hacksaw, screwdriver and left-handed monkey wrench!

All in all, restoring warbirds is a time-consuming and very expensive process. The finished products, however, are literally worth a fortune. Although unpublished, the latest selling price for a fully restored B-17 was rumored to be in the neighborhood of $4,500,000. In 1993, a *partial* fuselage and wing section for a German Me-109 fighter sold for $70,000. Since the Me-109 is quite rare, it will probably be worth over a million when fully restored.

Obviously, collecting and restoring warbirds is a hobby that very few can afford. Most specimens, restored and otherwise, now repose in museums scattered throughout the country.

Fortunately, a few non-profit organizations such as the Confederate and Yankee Air Forces are doing a magnificent job of preserving an important part of our aviation heritage.

Of the two, the CAF is the oldest and largest, dating back to the 1950s. It has wings and/or individual members in nearly all 50 states and carries a number of warbirds on its flying roster.

The small but growing YAF was founded at Willow Run Airport, Michigan, in 1981. The site was chosen due to its historical significance. During World War Two, Ford built over 8,000 B-24 Liberators at Willow Run. At the height of production, a finished Liberator rolled off the assembly line every 59 minutes. Of these, only three are to be found anywhere in the world today. In addition to its small but impressive roster of flying aircraft, the YAF also has a number of static (non-flying) warbirds on display at Willow Run.

When not flying on the air show circuit, most restored CAF and YAF warbirds are on display in the respective organizations' museums, where anyone can enjoy them. With luck, and the necessary financial support of philanthropists and the public, this situation should continue for many years to come.

In addition to the CAF and YAF museums, there are a number of private or government museums which are helping to preserve warbirds. The Champlin Fighter Museum in Mesa, Arizona, is devoted strictly to fighter aircraft, but their collection is an impressive one. In some cases, their World War One fighters are replicas built from scratch, as there were literally *no* known originals to be found anywhere in the world. While the use of replicas may be disappointing to purists, they're certainly better than no examples at all.

The Kellogg cereal manufacturers have contributed generously to the Kalamazoo Air Zoo in Kalamazoo, Michigan. The Air Zoo has an impressive roster of vintage aircraft and warbirds. Its nickname was inspired by the fact that it has an example of each of the famous Grumman "Cat" fighters, including the ultra-rare F7F Tigercat. During the summer months, visitors can tour the Air Zoo's restoration center and actually see what is involved in the restoration process.

Undoubtedly the oldest and largest organization which is helping to preserve our aviation heritage is the Experimental Aircraft Association. The EAA has several membership divisions, including warbirds, antiques, home-builts and experimental types from which it derives its name. The EAA's annual fly-in at Oshkosh, Wisconsin, is *the* aviation event of the year. Each summer, over 11,000 aircraft descend (no pun intended) on Oshkosh for the fly-in. The event attracts visitors from all over the world, and many return each year.

Unlike warbirds and other vintage aircraft, collecting and restoring old cars is a hobby which is within the financial reach of many mere mortals. An estimated 1,000,000 Americans collect, restore and exhibit old cars. If anything, that estimate is probably conservative.

Collectible cars fall into two classes, those which are merely collectible, and a much smaller number which are true classics. Further complicating the matter for beginners is the fact there are two distinct sets of standards for recognizing classics.

The Classic Car Club of America recognizes only certain models, and then only through the 1948 model year. In 1972, the Milestone Car Society established their own guidelines for classic cars. According to MCS, regardless of make or model year, a car may qualify as a classic if it's superior to its contemporaries in at least two of five categories. These are: styling, engineering, performance, innovation and craftsmanship. This standard is usually referred to as SEPIC for short. Some very rare and highly collectible cars don't make it as classics according to SEPIC standards; a few surprising ones do.

Although it may seem odd, scarcity isn't always a factor in old car values. Few people have ever heard of the Ford Model C, which may be the ultimate sleeper. Fewer than 30 Model C Cabriolets were produced, yet the few surviving examples are only worth about $15-20,000 in excellent condition. By contrast, two-seat Thunderbirds built between 1955 and 1957 are worth slightly more, even though over 53,000 were produced before the T-Bird degenerated into a four-seat model. (Blame *that* on Robert McNamara and his Whiz Kids, too.) The reason the early T-Birds are worth more than the much rarer model C is because more people *want* a two-seat Thunderbird.

Of course, *the* classic American car was the Duesenberg, of which fewer than 500 were manufactured during the 1930s. While base price was a whopping $11,000, most had custom features which boosted the average selling price to $18,000. That may be the average price for an American car today, but in the 1930s that same amount would have bought a very nice house, with money left over for a Cadillac in the garage. Today, a

Duesenberg in excellent condition is worth an estimated $175,000 or more.

Naturally, a verifiable association with a famous person will increase the value of any car. Al Capone's bullet-proof Cadillac or Hitler's Mercedes would obviously be worth many times the current market value of a comparable model without the name association. Ditto any of the more than 100 Cadillacs Elvis purchased during his lifetime, although whether the highest bidders would be actual car buffs or just rich Elvis fans is subject to conjecture.

With or without name association, the estimated values given are ball park figures only, based on averages. An example of any given model might sell for much more at a particularly spirited auction, or much less if the owner is desperate for a quick sale.

Unlike warbirds, many collectible cars can still be found at used car lots, or in junk yards. Despite its condemnation by Ralph Nader, the Chevy Corvair is a very popular and affordable collectible. One in restorable condition can often be found for as little as $1,500. "Restorable condition" simply means that all parts are there or can be readily found elsewhere. Replacement parts for older cars are also less of a problem than with warbirds. Of course, you can't just walk into the local Pep Boys and ask Manny, Moe or Jack for a fuel pump for a 1948 Tucker. It should be possible, however, to get one for a Corvair, older T-Bird or Mustang, many thousands of these cars are still on the road.

Complete restoration of many collectible models is well within the competence level of many back yard mechanics, although certain phases should be performed by experts. A friend of mine is presently restoring a Model T Ford, and the only job he plans to farm out is the final painting. Of course, he did have trouble finding a source for original axles in good condition. It seems they were quite popular as circus tent stakes during the 1930s and 1940s.

If you feel that restoring old cars is still beyond your mechanical or financial resources, there are numerous, smaller items which are well within the capabilities of most people. Several years ago, a friend of mine paid $10 for a shotgun which had gone through a flood. Although he knew virtually nothing about repairing or refinishing guns at the time, he decided to take a chance. He tackled the job with more enthusiasm than knowledge, and was amazed at the final result. Other than the finish, the gun had been virtually undamaged by the flood. He invested a few dollars in a refinishing kit, plus several hours' spare time. The end result was a beautifully refinished shotgun which is easily worth $200 or more on the used market.

Bear in mind that many antiques, old guns, cameras, etc., are actually worth more to collectors in average to good original condition than if they are refinished. An item which is in poor condition, however, might well be worth the time and effort it takes to restore it. Each item must be considered on an individual basis, but it shouldn't take too long to gain the experience necessary to determine if the effort would be worth it.

Fathoming The Unfathomable

No matter how experienced a person becomes at gauging the weather or reading a selling market, there will be some days they will "call" wrong. Sometimes, when viewed with the expert wisdom of hindsight, the reasons will be obvious. In other cases, it may be extremely difficult or even impossible to determine exactly why X occurred when it should have been Y. There may be a determining factor of which you are unaware, or it may simply be a variation of Murphy's Law at work. For those few who are unfamiliar with it, Murphy's Law states, "What can go wrong ... will."

This point was borne out all too clearly just last winter. My wife and I were planning to attend a wholesale gift show on Friday, which is always the slowest day of the show. A number of product reps would be idle and have time to talk to us whereas they would have people waiting in line on Saturday and Sunday. Another determining factor was the fact that our own sales at the swap meet are usually slowest on Friday.

As a hedge against bad weather on Saturday or Sunday, we went ahead and bought swap meet selling spaces for Friday. That way, if the weather was bad on one or two days the following weekend, we could forget the swap meet on whichever day it was the worst and attend the show then. If all three days were warm and sunny, we could call in temporary help to run an abbreviated setup for us on Friday.

Friday morning dawned cold and raw. The weather forecast called for a 50 percent chance of rain, which we considered a very conservative estimate. We called our helper and told her to stay home.

As we drove toward the show, we could see rain falling throughout the valley. What no one could predict at that point was that the rain would never reach the swap meet. When we polled several other vendors on Saturday morning, two or three said they had had the best Friday of the entire season. They were among the dozen or so vendors who decided to brave the weather, and thus had the handful of customers who came out all to themselves. Obviously, we shouldn't have canceled the temporary help, as she probably would have done quite well.

Based on the weather report, plus several other factors, our decision to simply write the day off was a sound one. It was the wrong one, but still sound. Given perfect weather, or even a cold day with no chance of rain, we would have done the exact opposite. It was the last weekend in January, just before many short-term snowbirds return home. They usually do their final shopping at the swap meet on Friday. That allows them to pack on Saturday and Sunday and be finished in time for the men to watch the Super Bowl Sunday afternoon. We knew this from past experience, but had simply forgotten it.

The whole weekend turned out to be weird. Our sales were decent enough Saturday, but Sunday was a disaster. Despite nice weather, neither our paperbacks (used) nor our Indian art (new) sold well. Our total sales for the day were about one-third what they had been on Saturday. Several other vendors reported roughly the same ratio. On virtually every other weekend of the month, Sunday had been our busiest day. I walked through the swap meet early Sunday afternoon, trying to read the crowd, which was fairly large. The only vendor who was actually busy was a "stuff" dealer who sold everything at close-out prices. Even though other "stuff" dealers were just standing around, the situation reminded me of one weekend several years ago. The "stuff" dealers were extremely busy on Saturday while those with high ticket jewelry or decorator items were busy just trying to stay awake. The following Saturday, the sales pattern did a 180 degree turn. The "stuff" dealers were complaining all day long, but the "class" dealers were too busy selling to listen to them.

The last-weekend-in-January syndrome applies again in the middle and at the end of March, only on a much larger scale. Since the majority of snowbirds leave on March 15th or 31st, the weekends immediately preceding those dates are usually extremely lucrative. Of course, Murphy likes to work overtime then, too. It invariably rains on one of those weekends, sometimes both. Last year, the mass exodus came at the end of March instead of after the 15th. Naturally, the weather was perfect the weekend preceding the 15th, but it rained two days out of three on the last weekend of the month.

By the last weekend of April, local residents outnumber snowbirds at the swap meet by at least four to one. The locals don't have much money, so sales are generally quite poor. Despite this thoroughly predictable situation, a friend of ours who sells high-ticket jewelry had her best day of the entire season at the end of April last year. There probably weren't more than 300 people at the swap meet during the entire day, which was blistering hot.

That figure did, however, include a bus load of Japanese tourists. Two or three of them were literally carrying duffel bags stuffed with cash, which they gladly donated to our friend's cash register. Would she work the last weekend of April at that location again? Definitely not! She realizes that bus load of Japanese just happened to be in the right place at the right time. The chances of it ever happening again on that weekend are extremely remote.

The above are perfect examples of selling situations which *should* be easily predictable, and usually are. Many seasoned, intelligent vendors are pretty good at calling them right 90 percent of the time. It's that other 10 percent that makes them want to try a different line of work!

Following are several examples of situations that seem to puzzle numerous vendors, whether they sell new or used goods. While most common to newcomers, they also apply to many who have been selling for years. The answers to some of them appear elsewhere in this book, but are important enough to bear repeating. Probable solutions, which appear in parentheses after each hypothetical problem, are so simple that I can't understand why more people can't see them for themselves. I know from experience, however, that many people simply can't recognize the obvious.

Fred started working the local swap meet, selling out of the trunk of his car. He sold so much on Friday and Saturday that he didn't have enough merchandise left for Sunday. He switched to his pickup, doubled his inventory, and still sold almost everything by Saturday afternoon. He doubled his inventory again, and increased his weekend gross sales 50 percent by being able to sell on

Sunday. When he doubled his inventory a third time, his sales increased only slightly. *Why?*

(Increasing inventory will increase sales proportionately only up to a certain point. Beyond that, doubling or even tripling may only produce a small increase in sales, if any. Unfortunately, it's impossible to determine that magic point beforehand. The old saying that a business either grows or fails is basically true, but expanding beyond the marketplace's ability to absorb the increase is equally bad. The best advice I can offer is this: When sales fail to keep pace with the increase in inventory, stop expanding and just try to maintain the present level until sales increase significantly.)

Recently, Nancy worked an arts and crafts show in a popular vacation area which contains numerous summer homes. Sales were so good that she worked another show in the same location two weeks later. Her sales were extremely poor at the second show. *Why?*

("Summer homes" is the key here. You can't sell to the same people twice in such a short time. It is possible to have successful shows back-to-back in a vacation area which had a constant turnover of tourists.)

Two weeks ago, the weather was beautiful. There was a large crowd at the swap meet, but sales were poor. Last week, the weather was bad and there were very few vendors or customers. Most vendors reported good to excellent sales. *Were they telling the truth?*

(They probably were. Generally speaking, a lot of browsers visit swap meets when the weather is good. Only serious customers go out in inclement weather. In some areas, the calendar will have a greater influence on sales than the weather. Sales will be good right after payday, poor on the weekend before. As mentioned earlier, sales are always best at our swap meet just before the snowbirds go home, regardless of the weather.)

Charlie had a lot of competition selling used books at the swap meet, so he decided to undercut everyone else. Before long, he was outselling all his competitors combined. *If he was selling so much, why did he go broke?*

(Charlie forgot that gross sales can be meaningless. It's the net that counts. That's spelled N-E-T, net profit. When Charlie lowered his prices too much, he also eliminated his profit. This problem is common to many larger vendors, who think they can outsell the competition by selling at the lowest price. Unfortunately, they don't just cut into their own profits. They take so many sales away from the competition that they can't make any money, either. They even create an impossible situation for non-competitors because customers soon expect everybody to give their merchandise away. My wife and I solve this problem by saying, "If you think our price is too high, lots of luck finding it elsewhere.")

Tom and Helen sell a variety of used goods at the swap meet. Some days they sell mostly tools, other days it's small appliances, dishware or toys. There doesn't seem to be a recognizable pattern, although their gross sales remain fairly consistent from day to day. *What causes this variation in buying patterns?*

(With few exceptions, no single item will sell consistently well every day at the same location. It's impossible to predict exactly what will sell on any given day, even with seasonal items. For this reason, a variety of merchandise is important. If overall sales are consistently good, don't worry about a variation in buying patterns.

Do try to phase out items which are consistently slow sellers and replace them with something that offers better potential.)

Bill sells used tools at the swap meet. His brother, Pete, sells the same thing at another swap meet several miles away. The customer base is virtually identical at both swap meets, yet Pete consistently outsells Bill each weekend. *Why?*

(It would be easy to say, "Some can sell 'em, some can't." This might very well be the case, but it isn't necessarily the only factor. The problem could be a difference in swap meets which is difficult to detect. Is the customer base of each *really* identical, or are there subtle differences? Pete might actually be more knowledgeable about tools, he might have a better personality, or he might just plain work harder at selling.

If possible, Bill should videotape both Pete and himself in typical selling situations. He should then view the tape and look for obvious differences in personality, sales technique and attitude. If Pete's presentation is obviously better, Bill should work on improving his own. If his is better than Pete's, and it may well be, the problem is probably a combination of location/merchandise. If location, it could be the swap meet itself, or Bill's location within it. He might do better by simply changing to a different row, preferably near an entrance or exit. If the problem is the merchandise, Bill has three options for change:

1. Cut prices drastically to liquidate his stock.
2. Sell the entire lot at a reduced price to another tool dealer.

3. Continue to sell tools at the regular price, but let his stock run down and replace it with other items until he finds the right combination.

Of the three options, the third is the least drastic, but will take the longest time to effect an increase in sales. Based on his own peculiar set of circumstances, only Bill can decide which option is best.)

Don't Be A Muddlethrough

When my wife and I returned to our winter market last year, we found that a number of changes had been made during the summer. Most were for the benefit of the owners, not the customers and vendors.

In previous years, there had been a $1 per car charge for parking, but admission to the swap meet itself was free. Now, parking was free, but there was a charge of 50 cents per person to enter the swap meet. The owners had fenced off the grounds, so customers were forced to enter through four controlled gates, rather than via the aisle nearest to where they had parked. The fence also played havoc with lines of vendors trying to enter through the two vendor gates, then maneuver into their selling spaces. Many were forced to arrive an hour earlier than in previous years just to ensure they *could* get into their spaces.

While the admission charge was obviously the same as before for one couple in a vehicle, it was more for a car load of people. As a protest, many snowbirds boycotted the swap meet, even going so far as to put up notices in the laundry rooms of the RV parks where they lived. The boycott eliminated a lot of casual browsers, but it also reduced the number of serious shoppers. Needless to say, quite a few vendors experienced a drastic reduction in sales.

After one particularly discouraging weekend, a friend of ours called and predicted the swap meet was a dying market. "A lot of dealers are off sixty to seventy percent," he wailed. *"Sixty to seventy percent."*

Since our sales had been good the preceding weekend, my wife countered with our favorite response to such a gloomy outlook. "What do they sell?" she asked. "Probably the same thing they sold last year, or even ten years ago. Don't they know they have to make some changes from year to year? It's a constantly shifting marketplace."

"Of course their sales are down," I added, "they're all Muddlethroughs."

While those simple statements may not reveal the wisdom of the ages, they do pretty well summarize the basic differences between those who succeed and those who fail. This is true in both the business world and in everyday life. A *lot* of people are Muddlethroughs. They stumble through life with the minimum effort required to just get by. Some are doubtless hindered by poor health or limited mental capacity, but the majority of Muddlethroughs are just plain *lazy*. They find it much easier to complain about their station in life than to work to improve it.

We have a friend who could easily be one of the most successful vendors in the business, but she has a real problem. She considers "work" to be the dirtiest, vilest, most horrifying word in the English language. She's quite intelligent and a natural salesperson, but she goes out of her way to avoid anything she believes even remotely resembles work. In fact, I'm sure she works harder at trying *not* to work than she would if she actually worked. Consequently, her sales are far less than outstanding and definitely well below her true potential. In short, she's a Muddlethrough.

Although we have known quite a few Muddlethroughs over the years, I didn't coin the term until a couple of years ago. It was summer, and we were working a swap meet located a couple of hours from home. Unlike the situation at our winter market, business was pretty good despite the heat. While working there, we met a couple who liked to brag about some of the markets they had worked in previous years. Their bragging usually centered around the thousands of dollars they grossed each weekend. We certainly didn't see any evidence of their supposed past successes.

As we watched them over the course of two or three weekends, we began to wonder how they could have achieved any degree of success at *anything*. Despite the fact they had supposedly been in the business for years, they seemed to function strictly on the most inexperienced, amateur level. We never did know their last name, but I nicknamed them Mr. and Mrs. Muddlethrough because they just seemed to be muddling through from one day to the next. Since that time, I have applied the title to quite a few people. A few examples of just how Muddlethroughs operate will suffice. Bear in mind that not all these examples are based on the original Muddlethroughs, but several are.

Although there were usually three people working the Muddlethroughs' stand, usually only Mrs. Muddlethrough carried any change. If she went to the rest room or the snack bar, she would neglect to leave any with her husband or daughter. If they needed to make change while she was gone, guess who they asked. That's right, my wife and I were set up right next to them, so they came to us. I know Mrs. Muddlethrough actually *had* change, because she always brought ours back to us as soon as she returned. Why couldn't she have simply left some with her husband and daughter? Better yet, why didn't *each* of them have at least some change to begin with? It's not unusual on a busy selling day for three or four people working a single stand to be making sales and needing change at the same time.

Even vendors who normally carry plenty of change can run short occasionally, but Muddlethroughs *never* seem to carry enough, if any. I've lost track of the number of times that a so-called professional vendor has asked us to break a twenty at the start of the selling day. In one case, it was the *same* vendor several weeks in a row. We did it the first couple of times, but when they started making a practice of it, we simply told them we were short ourselves. In one case, a vendor admitted he had $300 in his wallet, but it was three $100 bills. Why didn't he get at least one of them changed at the bank earlier in the day? The only answer I can offer is that he's a Muddlethrough.

On the first rainy day we were set up next to Mr. and Mrs. Muddlethrough, we saw just how ill-prepared they were for inclement weather. When they saw us covering our merchandise with large sheets of clear plastic, they ran over and asked if we had any extras they could borrow. We did, and gladly loaned them some. However, we were a little chagrined when they returned them later. They had simply wadded up the sheets while they were still wet, yet it would have taken only a couple of minutes to hang them in the sun to dry.

At the swap meet where we met the Muddlethroughs, most regular vendors who had canopies simply closed them in at night and left their merchandise inside. When it came time to close, the Muddlethroughs didn't have extra tarps for the purpose. They had to pull the top off their canopy and use it. Naturally, they managed to knock merchandise off their tables and sustain a certain amount of breakage. The losses they suffered in just a couple of weekends would have more than paid for the extra tarps necessary to secure the front and sides of their setup.

Most vendors try to standardize the size of their packing boxes to simplify loading and unloading, but not the Muddlethroughs. Their box sizes would vary from week to week, so they were never able to pack their van the some way twice in a row. One or two trips to the supermarket would have furnished all the apple, orange or banana boxes they needed to standardize their packing procedure. When we suggested this, they thought it was a good idea, but they never followed through on it. *That* would have required a little extra effort.

Perhaps their biggest mistake of all, though, was in not making any significant changes in their merchandise. They sold toys, custom license plates and watches, just like several other vendors at the same swap meet. Naturally, their sales were affected accordingly. Rather than trying something new, they continued to restock the items which didn't sell well. Making changes would have required a little extra effort, but the potential for increased sales would have made that effort worthwhile. Of course, if they wanted to know what time it was, they asked us. Although they sold watches, none of them wore one!

My wife and I still sell the one basic item we started with eight years ago, but we've reduced our inventory of it drastically. It continues to sell reasonably well, but we can no longer count on it for a living. We constantly add new items and drop old ones which no longer sell, even if it means closing them out at below our cost. Our theory is that an item which cost us $20 but isn't selling is actually worth nothing to us. If we sell it for $15, that's $15 we can put into something that *will* sell.

Several months ago, we decided to weed out our paperback book setup. After two years in the business, we had learned that certain authors and titles might be extremely popular one year, but sell very poorly the next. We traded off the slow sellers and replaced them with new favorites or perennial best sellers. Sure, we went "Ouch!" at the thought of having to trade two of our books for every used book of equal value to one of ours, and in some cases having to pay some cash in addition, but the bottom line is we were able to upgrade our inventory and increase sales.

We know a number of other vendors who also make changes from time to time. Some sell only new goods, some sell used, and a few sell a combination of the two. We also know quite a few others who haven't changed their inventory in years. Invariably, they're the ones who complain the most about sales being down. They simply don't realize that an item which was popular last year, or several years ago, may not be popular today. Instead, they just muddle through and complain about how bad business is without seeking a solution to their problem.

It takes time and energy to seek out new merchandise, selling techniques and markets. Even then, success isn't automatically assured. It may be necessary to make several changes before hitting on the right combination. The effort can, however, produce positive results well beyond your expectations.

Earlier, I mentioned the fact that the new fence at our winter market played havoc with some vendors trying to maneuver their vehicles into their selling spaces. As a solution, most began arriving earlier than in previous years. Naturally, the Muddlethrough who sets up across from us does exactly the opposite. Whereas he used to arrive around 7:00 AM or shortly thereafter, he now seldom arrived before 9:00. It would be hilarious watching him try to maneuver into his space if it wasn't so pathetic. As it is, he has to drive up one aisle, then down another until he can find a place to turn and make a semi-direct approach to his space. Even though he drives a compact station wagon and *should* be able to make the turns, he still manages to run into other vendors' tables and knock their merchandise to the ground. When he finally gets out of his car, I almost expect him to start feeling his way about with a white cane.

Over the years, I've seen quite a few Muddlethroughs arrive late, then expect other vendors to move tables, canopies, etc., so they will have room to maneuver into their space. More often than not, they're driving an oversized van or pickup, making it virtually impossible to get into their space. When that happens, they're forced to leave their vehicle in the aisle while they unload. If they arrive late enough, this interrupts the traffic flow of customers. Needless to say, this practice costs their neighbors sales and makes them *very* unpopular. I can understand it happening to a rank amateur who doesn't realize just how early customers arrive, but it's inexcusable for so-called professionals who work the swap meet on a regular basis. Yet some of them are repeat offenders, arriving late day after day.

While most Muddlethroughs appear to be lazy, stupid, or both, such isn't always the case. A few are simply victims of inexperience and ignorance. Fortunately, both of these shortcomings can be corrected.

About the time we met the original Muddlethroughs, we also met a couple of ladies who were brand new in the business. They had nice merchandise, but weren't displaying it effectively. My wife suggested several ways in which they could improve their display. They implemented her suggestions the following day. When she made additional suggestions, they also followed through on those. In short, they weren't afraid to admit their ignorance and were willing to take some advice from a seasoned pro. We haven't seen them for a couple of years, but hope they were successful in their efforts. They were making a sincere effort to do everything right and deserve to succeed.

As the bottom line, if you want to ensure failure, or at the most success in spite of yourself, become a Muddlethrough. You will certainly have plenty of company. If you want to succeed, then expend the extra time and effort necessary to increase your chances. There may be plenty of competition to reach the top, but it isn't crowded once you get there.

The Last Word

Whether selling new goods or used, the information contained in the preceding chapters has enabled numerous individuals to achieve success. Applied properly, the principles and techniques should work equally well for you.

However, if I've learned anything from several years in the business, it's that no two individuals are alike. What works well for one might not work at all for another. At some point, you may decide to try something totally contrary to what I recommend. If it works for you, and you make money at it, just keep on doing it until it no longer works. If that time never comes, so much the better. After all, there is no argument that refutes success —period.

YOU WILL ALSO WANT TO READ:

☐ **64145 SHADOW MERCHANTS: Successful Retailing Without a Storefront,** *by Jordan Cooper.* How to make money in low-overhead, streetcorner style operations by someone who's been there. This book covers Swap Meets; Flea Markets; Streetcorners; Arts & Crafts Shows; Mall Kiosks; Fairs and Carnivals; Gun Shows; And much more. It also includes valuable advice on pitfalls to avoid. *1993, 5½ x 8½, 152 pp, illustrated, soft cover.* $12.95.

☐ **13077 HOW TO MAKE CASH MONEY SELLING AT SWAP MEETS, FLEA MARKETS, ETC.,** *by Jordan Cooper.* After years of making good money at flea markets, the author lets you in on the secrets of success. What to Sell; Transportation; Setting-up; How to Display Your Wares; Pricing; Advertising; Rain and Bad Weather; The IRS; And much more. *1988, 5½ x 8½, 180 pp, illustrated, soft cover.* $14.95.

☐ **14099 THE ART & SCIENCE OF DUMPSTER DIVING,** *by John Hoffman.* This book will show you how to get just about *anything* you want or need — food, clothing, furniture, building materials, entertainment, luxury goods, tools, toys — you name it — *ABSOLUTELY FREE!* Take a guided tour of America's back alleys where amazing wealth is carelessly discarded. Hoffman will show you where to find the good stuff, how to rescue it and how to use it. *1993, 8½ x 11, 152 pp, illustrated, soft cover.* $12.95.

··

Loompanics Unlimited
PO Box 1197
Port Townsend, WA 98368   **SHS94**

Please send me the books I have checked above. I have enclosed $_____ which includes $4.00 for shipping and handling of 1 to 3 books, $6.00 for 4 or more. Washington residents include 7.9% sales tax.

Name _____

Address _____

City/State/Zip _____

We now accept Visa and MasterCard.
Credit Card orders *only* call 1-800-380-2230.